MICS! CAMERA! ACTION!

An Insider's Guide to Becoming a Media Star!

Written by:
MARC FREDEN

With a Generous Contribution From:
NIKIJHA "First Lady Niki" LYNCH

ISBN-13: 979-8-9889123-9-2 paperback
ISBN-13: 979-8-9889123-8-5 ebook

Library of Congress Control Number: 2023915999
For permission requests, write to the publisher, addressed "Attention: Permissions Coordinator," at the address below:
marc.freden@gmail.com

ACKNOWLEDGEMENT

We would like to acknowledge the numerous professionals who contributed to the "SIDEBAR" segments of the book and the multiple celebrities who unwittingly contributed to the anecdotal stories which added to this book's entertainment factor.

We must acknowledge our editor, Rachelle Jones, for her keen observations and attention to detail. Also, we would like to give notice to James Messer for his cover design and Toula Mavridou Messer without whose initial inspiration and encouragement this book would never have come about.

Finally, we must pay tribute to the hundreds of colleagues along the way who shaped our experiences and forwarded our careers. They are as much a part of our success as our own hard work. They are between every written line of this book.

TABLE OF CONTENTS

PREFACE

WHY THIS BOOK...NOW?

This book is not a luxury...it's a necessity. Why? Media runs the business, generates sales, is the news, fluctuates the economy, changes opinion, is political, gives voice, sends messages, sets trends, spreads gossip, and allows the individual a worldwide platform. From traditional outlets, such as television and radio, to social media and even personal appearances; knowing how to appear in public should be part of your career training. Marketing everything from businesses, to personal skill sets, to your resume, happens in one shape or form, these days, using a form of media. Even the least savvy of you now applies for jobs via the internet and getting a job generally involves a background check of your social media footprint. You should be prepared for whether you want to be in it...or need to be in it.

Knowing what you are doing, using the tools correctly, and putting your best face forward are the difference between success and failure in a competitive world. And if you are thinking not everything is a competition...think again. Whether you are beating the competition in business, promoting your new cookbook and chef skills, trying to be a social influencer, being a social commentator, or swiping right for the right date; you are selling yourself—de facto trying to find the edge over the competition. Many jobs and careers expect you to self-promote on some sort of social platform. Remote or distance work scenarios and meetings are more and more the norm. In doing so, we make presentations, we represent the company, our boss, and ourselves and why would we not want to do that in the best possible light?

And, quite simply, many of us just really have something to say. Using the media, in many of its different incarnations, gives a voice to the

previously mute. Again, knowing how to do this, correctly, professionally, with personality and presence is key to success—a.k.a. being
seen and heard.

This book breaks down five different but interlocking aspects of media
as it pertains to the art of communication:

- TELEVISION
- RADIO
- PODCASTS
- SOCIAL MEDIA
- PUBLIC SPEAKING

By understanding the elements of "how to…" within each craft, you
will see factors that help in all aspects of the public "you." In other
words, pulling from the lessons learned in the TELEVISION and RADIO
sections which follow, inevitably will help shape you when defining
the person and product you want to create in the PODCAST, SOCIAL
MEDIA, and PUBLIC SPEAKING segments of the book.

MICS! CAMERA! ACTION! is a comprehensive compendium of career
experiences that you won't have learned in the classroom—but in the
field, on the road, in the studio, on-camera, and behind the scenes.
They aren't secrets, they are learned truths. And the truth is: if you
want or need to be in the media spotlight for any reason, the following isn't just what you want to know…it is what you need to know.

SO, WHO ARE WE?
MARC FREDEN:

Forty years…and then some. Sure, there are nearly four decades of professional experience including writing, producing, editing, directing, teaching, developing, and a decade or so on-camera. Still, Marc Freden can trace the start of his entertainment career on the stages of summer stock and regional theater and dance studios as a child actor. He never knew a time when he wasn't driven to be in the entertainment business.

"I liken my entertainment career to that of a tree," Freden explains the diversity of his resume. "Sometimes I sat on the branch of being an author. Sometimes I sat on the branch of being an entertainment journalist. Sometimes I sat on the branch of being a television producer. And so, it goes. But as different as every job has been, it has never been off the entertainment tree."

As comfortable in front of the camera as he is behind the scenes, Freden now finds comfort in front of the keyboard having published two in his series of the "Dark Side of the Bright Lights" novels, NOT TOO COCKSURE and HEIR LINE FRACTURE (Sunstone Press © 2015) and the soon to be published SCANDAL EYES exposing the dark secrets from Hollywood and the world of celebrity. Already acclaimed as an author for his autobiographical "REALLY!?!—A Memoir and Other Observations from a Man Who's Lived Life 'Not Quite Famous Enough'" in which his witty and sardonic take on the world around him has garnered praise from the esteemed Publishers Weekly: "Freden's energy, charisma, and honesty are admirable; readers will come away rooting for him to become 'famous enough.'"

Freden has also concentrated his considerable skills through his own On The Marc Creative, developing several pilot presentations for varied genres of television and entertainment—for both the U.K. and American markets. Freden has also been tapped as an adjunct professor at the Laureate and SAE international schools, teaching his unique approach to video/film/television production to the next generation of creative minds.

Freden's production credits have taken him from some of the most exciting red carpets in the entertainment world to behind the scenes on some of the most impressive films and television series ever created; interviewed the biggest names in show business and worked for such notable networks as NBC, ABC, Bravo, MTv, E! and Reelz. Freden has also contributed to the successful electronic press kit marketing of over 20 feature films including: "Rain Man", "Torch Song Trilogy", "Bright Lights Big City", "Biloxi Blues" and "Nightmare on Elm Street IV".

As an on-camera talent, American audiences first came to know Freden's adept 'turn-of-phase' writing and quick-witted personality on the syndicated series "Extra". Later, Freden was a reporter for the MGM series "Uncovered" and as a guest commentator for VH1 and A&E's "Biography". But it was during his tenure as bureau chief for Britain's highest-rated morning news magazine program, "GMTV", Freden created a career achieved by few in television— steady work on two continents. Freden broke ground as the very first American correspondent contracted to a news series in British television history. And he soon proved to be well worth the risk—not just another 'Hollywood insider' but a genuine television 'personality'—unique, witty, irreverent, factual...and always entertaining.

NIKIJHA "FIRST LADY NIKI" LYNCH:

Sassy and sweet, urban and urbane, outspoken and spoken about; Nikijha Lynch has earned her radio moniker as "First Lady Niki" the old-fashioned way: with a voice, an opinion, a point of view, and a loyalty—to her profession, to her audience. It's a winning combination that has been successful for more than two decades. Not bad for the local gal who never thought of getting into radio...but let radio get into her.

Lynch's start may have been inauspicious, but it was certainly fortuitous. She answered an ad for a competition to find a new and different radio news reader. And winning was just the beginning. Beginning with a fifteen-year odyssey with iHeart radio, Niki honed her on-air multi-facets on everything from a morning show co-host to a solo midday personality. Knowing that fans come first, "First Lady Niki" became a regular for live remote broadcasts, public appearances, and weekly club dates. Segueing to Sun Broadcasting in 2016, Niki is a hit on Fort Myers, Florida, FLY 98.5, where she handles the double duties of morning drive and midday broadcasts.

Along with her radio obligations, First Lady Niki is first with community relations working closely with non-profit organizations to broaden their awareness within the community and beyond. Having been self-taught in the industry, she has collected considerable knowledge of the industry's ins and outs. She is now a much sought-after consultant for those up-and-comers looking to break into the industry.

"I look for innate talent. You can't teach someone to be a natural. I look at the talent I work with as diamonds in the rough. I start to facet them, and they will sparkle. But they have to start as a natural gem," Nikijha explains about her coaching philosophy. "I don't believe in crushing dreams, but I do work in reality. Still, just like a diamond in the rough...you are ostensibly creating something beautiful out of what is just a rock. So, rock on!"

A FEW WORDS FROM A COUPLE OF PEOPLE WHO HAVE BEEN THERE...AND DONE THAT:

I'VE BEEN IN THE ROOM WHEN:

I'll be frank; the media can be a rough business—harsh and unfair. Breaking in requires tough skin and resilience. Even amateur videos on YouTube can be subject to mean-spirited critique. Some of which can make it, go viral and yesterday's embarrassing moment is suddenly tomorrow's success story. It's a strange business in that way. (Think about the Gangnam Style video and the sensation that it caused.)

But I have been there when vital decisions were made by cruel impressions and careers were changed by it. Mine included. I will take you back to the launch of EXTRA—the syndicated entertainment news series. I was on the original team developing the show. And one weekend during the summer, while still in development and before our September launch date, all the management, producers, and talent, me included, were invited to a picnic at a beach in Santa Barbara, California, near the home of the show's creator, David Newell. At the event, was Gerald Levin the head of the then corporate entity TIME/WARNER, the parent company of the show, who, incidentally, mentioned to me that he "liked my work." High praise indeed.

As the day went on, Arthel Neville arrived. She was the co-host and daughter of one of the famed Neville Brothers' singing clan. I was standing with Newell, Levin, and a few management folks when the other co-host arrived. I will not state his name for privacy purposes with this particular story, but everyone was very excited to see whom he was bringing to the event as a date. He was strikingly handsome, with model good looks and a booming baritone voice—the white Adonis and a perfect anchorman. Arthel, at the time, was engaged to a professional football player who was there in attendance. And the anchorman had only been overheard professing love over the cell phone the night before after a retreat dinner. So curiosity was high as to whom the lovely lady would be.

He arrived just late enough for an audience to gather. And who stepped out of the passenger seat but a gorgeous...black male! With-out missing a beat, Levin turned to all present and announced: "We are not launching an $80-million-dollar show with a black woman and a gay man! Fix it!" Within days and just shy of our launch, the an-chorman was replaced.

Over the course of the next many months, the show went through in-carnations and re-development, which gave management the excuse to fire all the on-camera males who were gay—me included.

I tell you this because just a few years later, I was hired in London as the first correspondent/presenter ever contracted to a British news show in British television history. The show was called GMTV, and it was the British equivalent of TODAY or GOOD MORNING AMERICA. What eventually won them over? "You're as camp as Christmas," I was told by my managing editor. In other words—or British speak—they loved the fact that I am gay. Go figure.

I have been in the room when people are talking about me. Ques-tions were flying: "Is he too tall?... too short?...too fat?...too thin?... too funny?...too serious?...too young?...too old?... TOO MUCH?" I even pointed out that I was in the room and that I could hear them talking. No one flinched. Because they were not talking about me, they were talking about a product they needed. And I knew right there and then there were two Marc Fredens: the product and the person. When people criticize or put a subjective value on my work, they are talking about a product…not the person. Does that product sell the message? It allowed me to absorb criticism constructively and not as a personally destructive attack. There are plenty of times I would not have cast myself, as the product, in a role or position even though I know the person was fully capable of handling the job at hand. I have even seen a casting notice for which they were looking for a "Marc Freden type" and I didn't get the job. Go figure. They weren't looking for me, just someone who had my qualifications—the product of me. That is when you know you can be objective about your qualifications and qualities. Don't limit yourself. Just know what the product is best for.

In understanding the dichotomy of being a product versus a person, I can't condone the discriminatory practice of being fired for being gay but can better see why Gerald Levin was concerned with the presumed viewer backlash of the product placement of a black woman and gay male anchor team launching a high-profile series and the radical publicity, at the time, it could have generated. Was America ready for that "product" in their home?

I say all this because, as you venture into the world of media for whatever your personal or professional reasons, remember to define the product you will become. Separate that product from the person you are, and you will save yourself from the emotional distress of criticism. Recognized the product is not right for everything, everywhere. But hone that product to the best of its abilities.

This book is about developing that product on many platforms, in many ways, by giving practical advice—not just "how to…" but also "why to…" which comes from years of having been it and done it.

—Marc Freden

URBAN RENEWAL:

"What is meant for me, will be!" Those were the words I spoke to myself before I walked into the staff meeting. They, the management, had been looking for the perfect voice, the perfect personality, for the very day part for which I had been filling in "temporarily" for months. This was the meeting in which they were to declare the position filled. Needless to say, I was the heir apparent. The meeting begins, and the station manager announces a new hire, which wasn't me, to fill the slot. He went on to explain why—stating that while he had considered me, I was "too urban." Those were words I'll never forget. Those were the days when, even as a black woman, you didn't pull the race card; and I had to collect the thoughts in my head, trying to believe that maybe it just wasn't my time. I wasn't just disappointed but, more so, taken aback by the words "too urban." Just what did he mean by that?

The decision and statement left a few of my colleagues disappointed and slightly stunned as well.

As the meeting dismissed, I walked down the hall with one of my colleagues whom I also considered a friend. He expressed that he wasn't pleased with the choice. I told him what I had told myself earlier that day: "What›s meant for me will be, and no one can take that away.» He knew I was upset but was going to remain silent. He, on the other hand, wasn't about to be. To his credit, he voiced what I didn't, but things got so heated that it led to his suspension. I can only imagine what would have been in it for me. I hated that it happened to him yet, I appreciated that he was willing to fight and stand up for what and whom he believed in!

I took my eyes off the «position,» and focused on the person, ME! I was going to hone my craft, and be at the top of my game! While do-ing so, that statement never left my mind: «She›s too urban.» I started to think about it in context; not about me, but about the personality behind the mic. And although it could have been said differently, I began to understand the message. Early on my speech was relaxed and filled with colloquialisms...a kind of urbanization of conversation. While I thought the way I was communicating was being «true to myself"—something that is so much easier to do and far more accepted today—I had to understand and realize I wasn›t just chatting with my girlfriends over the airwaves. When we chat with our friends we use shortcuts and familiar phrases that don't translate to the larger audience. I was talking to that larger audience, filled with hundreds of thousands of people that needed to understand what I was saying—not groping through the urban dictionary to understand what I was saying. My thoughts moved away from «I›ll show them to I›ll show myself that I can do this!»

A short time later comes a major hurricane. People needed information from someone from the community who spoke their language, and who could understand what was happening to them because they lived with them and knew the mood and tone of the city. The newly brought-in talent was quite literally a fish out of water. So, who do they need to lean on? The girl who was «too urban.» At this critical time, I was going live daily and, with the help of one of my fellow morning show co-hosts, leading the way. I quickly learned the mechanics of radio—how to skillfully operate the board (control panel) for live broadcasts, how to time out content and deliver clear and concise messaging to the listening audience. Even though we were all in this together, management took notice. I was quickly going from being "too urban" to the "urbanator!"

Once things settled, we returned to regular programming, and I moved away from double duty. Only a few years in, I knew I was on to something. I knew that this was a space that I was meant to occupy! Things began to flow! Then BOOM, here we go again, another issue with the talent that filled that day part. This time around the conversation was a little different, it came with a job offer and an apology saying: « I think I made a mistake." The more he listened, he saw the growth and felt like I was the right fit for the job! Even after all I had gone through, I still didn›t know if I was ready to accept the job because the success of it would solely be on my shoulders. Even though I was proud of myself for how far I had come, it was still scary. Especially with the negative voices around me echoing words like it›s «impossible» to do what you›re trying to do in such a short amount of time. The louder the voices got, the more I said to myself, «WATCH THIS," and decided to lean into new possibilities. I›m so glad I did! I realize now, that if I had fought, as my friend had done on my behalf—even if the cause was right—I would have lost the battle and probably be out before I began. A pyrrhic victory but not a resume builder. Today I know that initial kick in the ass was a boost up the ladder...and I am grateful for a twenty-plus year career as "The First Lady Niki!"

—Nikijha Lynch

WHAT ARE YOU IN FOR?
EFFORT, WORK...COMMITMENT

Success in all forms of media—whether you are trying to make a living from it or maintain a presence as a spokesperson for business, branding, or personal messaging—takes work. This will not come by accident. Your "need" for the media may be from an accidental occurrence, but your expertise in usage will come from knowledge of how it works and how to work it. All of which takes commitment. This isn't something you try...this is something you make happen. We can tell you how and why, but only you know what is in it for you. So if you are ready...read on.

TELEVISION

TELEVISION

PART ONE:

WHAT ARE YOU TRYING TO ACHIEVE?

Let's start with a simple fact. The business of show business isn't easy. As they say, if It was everyone would be doing it. Although it seems these days, everyone does have a toe in the water. Why not? Opportunity is everywhere. But fame and fortune are elusive. The first understanding you should take away is this is not SHOW business...it is show BUSINESS. Entertainment is the business of show, and you need to treat it as a business no matter what aspect in which you are trying to broach. Television is the most obvious, most omnipresent, and is a worldwide opportunity waiting to be conquered. These days there are several avenues: traditional terrestrial television, cable television, streaming, and the internet all vying for market share and your waning attention span.

More and more, you hear young people say, "I don't watch television!" Ah, but they do. Just because they get their entertainment fix on a laptop, tablet, or phone instead of a flat screen in the family living room doesn't mean they're not watching television. And just because they are not watching what used to be known as the big three networks (ABC, NBC, and CBS) and instead are only watching subscription-based streamers like Paramount + or HBO Max also doesn't mean they aren't watching television. And yes, even a YouTube channel is considered television. Television is defined as a system for transmitting visual images and sounds (entertainment, information, or education) that are reproduced on screens (any device). So surprise, television is alive and well and just as popular as ever...and I dare say, more people are trying to utilize the industry than ever—be it a career choice or just marketing viral videos, people are turning to TV to create a career.

FAME OR FORTUNE? WHY NOT...

I will go out a limb and say the Kardashians ruined it for everyone. They made it look too easy to turn a lack of obvious talent into a billion-dollar enterprise. Now, everyone wants in. What did they have that most people don't: business savvy and commitment.

Before there were the Kardashians, there was Paris Hilton, who turned a dimwitted persona on television's THE SIMPLE LIFE and a trademarked catchphrase "That's hot!" into a household must-watch, vicarious, sensation. She had the name, she had the wealth, but she only had one note. The Kardashians simply took it five times further— five sisters and manipulative 'momanger' to create opportunity where there was none. Making something out of nothing and convincing the world the 'emperor had a closet full of new clothes' was part of the game. Fans watched, believed, copied, emulated, were inspired by... and the 'influencer' opportunity took off. I'm not saying the Kardashians created the influencer marketplace, but they certainly fueled the fire of niche branding and influence money making as a lesson for all to follow.

But there have always been these types of insta-celebrities and focus-driven personalities who appear to be little more than famous for being famous. Decades before the Kardashians and the Hiltons (including Paris' sister Nikki in the mix) there were the glamorous Gabor sisters, Zsa Zsa and Eva, b-list actresses and society figure Hungarian émigrés who never lost their accents or charms and were the delight of the talk show circuit. Zsa Zsa famously claimed to be a housekeeper when asked about her wealth, explaining: "I marry, I get divorced, I keep the house." Those kinds of witticisms kept the public wondering just what the truth was about these two Hollywood phenoms...therefore keeping the public wanting more.

I'M GOING TO SAY IT AGAIN... COMMITMENT

And that is the bottom line. It takes commitment. You don't just become an overnight success—although anyone's video can go viral, audition tapes can be picked up or the right pair of eyes or ears can spot your talents—you must maintain to sustain. Do you have the energy, the time, the business plan, content, drive, or willingness it takes to put in what you need to get out what you want? If you have read this far, I want to believe you do. But I will caution you from the start, your commitment had better be more about passion than purse strings, at least initially; otherwise, you are bound to be grossly disappointed.

As we move forward, you will find your niche, define your strengths, settle on a platform, develop content, refine your voice, and create market opportunity. That is the process. There is no sidestep; there is no shortcut. There is work to do. There is, fortunately, no shortage of clever people with clever ideas, and presumably, you are one of them. I would say just jump in and get started...but I caution you to have a plan.

- What do you want to achieve?
  - ◊ Define your end goal personally and professionally.

- What do you expect to achieve?
  - ◊ Is it monetary?

  - ◊ Is the growth of a business?

◊   Is it to promote a product or talent?

- Can you reasonably expect to achieve it from where you are starting?

    ◊   Do you have sustainable content to achieve your goal?

    ◊   Do you have the education, talent, or expertise to reach that goal?

    ◊   Does it require financing or a great deal of time (time is money)?

CAN YOU MAKE MONEY?

This is what you want to know…right?

First, you may want to think again if you are getting into the news business to get rich. Traditional jobs, such as reporters at traditional outlets will receive payment associated with the size of the market. We refer to the early days of a reporter's career as a 'news gypsy' as they may be making many moves from market to market as they climb the ranks from the market size or prestige positions such as a weekend anchor or main anchor. Again, these jobs are about passion, not a paycheck. At least initially, until you prove your worth and/ or define your individuality as a valued entity. But life and career experience mean something. And many seasoned journalists write books, go on the lecture circuit or become college professors to earn supplemental income. Similarly, your skills as a journalist are invaluable should you change gears as platforms change, television and news gathering evolves to new platforms and formats. The future is right around the corner, and you never know what opportunities can evolve. Peripheral vision is just as important as laser focus in your career.

As far as non-traditional platforms such as social media financial opportunities, we will explore and break down how that works in the
SOCIAL MEDIA segment of this book. Suffice it to say, there is a lucrative opportunity that takes a great deal of work. You don't just come
up with an idea, put it on a YouTube channel, and hope it takes off.
There is constant marketing, interplay with other social media platforms, cultivating followers, cultivating branding, etc. to reach mini-
mal goals for financial payouts. It's doable and exciting and should
not be discouraged. Understanding the marketplace is the difference
between just having a good idea and having the right idea. Research
is key.

What is truly exciting about today's platforms and marketplace is
that there is room for good ideas—be it personal exploitation such as
stand-up comedy or an original album release; a source for commentary or editorial speech; artistic expressions such as painting, cooking,
or music videos; or even scripted series. Equipment is inexpensive,
editing is user friendly, platforms are available, marketable, and viewer popular. The right product in the right space has the real possibility
of going viral in today's viewer-hungry world. That one product may
not make you money, but its popularity could turn the creator (you)
into a desired or sort-after content producer which can create income
streams in 'gun-for-hire- opportunities or in subsequent viral videos.

PART TWO:

AVENUES:

Television presents a world of opportunity these days—for both the traditionally trained, college-educated communications degree holder to the TikTok or YouTuber amateur about to go viral. Each presents possibilities and pitfalls.   The following highlights different opportunities within today's television marketplace:

REPORTER/JOURNALIST

- DEFINE JOURNALIST
  A journalist is defined as an occupation reporting news or current events. Traditionally, this is a career that occurs within newsrooms of network affiliates and requires training or schooling.

  - ◊ HARD NEWS
    From breaking news to a 'day turn', the hard news reporter is on the beat of working on what is happening based on the day's assignment. What is happening at the time is 'newsworthy' and timely. There is a news cycle whereby a story breaks and subsequently becomes stale if it is not told within a certain time frame. Hard news is generally stories that a driven by subject matter such as crime, politics, tragedy, and disaster—both locally and nationally.

◊   NICHE
This beat is human interest both in hard news and soft:

- Hard news: War Correspondent, Economics, Sports

- Soft news: Arts and Entertainment, Lifestyles

- CAN YOU CREATE YOUR VOICE?
"Talk" on television has never been more prolific—from 24-hour news channels to parody news series to niche reporters and internet influencers; there are commentators and life observers. And those are who I particularly want to focus on, the life observers. A news channel such as FOX or MSNBC can give you a platform to rant and either you agree or disagree but that is just commentary. In those cases, it's a skill but not a craft. Those life observers find the nuggets in society, the oddities if you will, and craft an interesting story around it. Telling stories rather than simply relaying the events is a rare opportunity in the business of reporting. Two remarkable individuals who have created superlative and lasting careers by finding a voice in crafting emotional, humorous, eclectic, heartwarming, oddball, or simply overlooked stories within everyday life—elevating the ordinary to the extraordinary are:

- CNN's JEANNE MOOS:
With an acerbic quick wit and the ability to turn a phrase Moos has turned the most obscure of subject matter into riveting television segments under such notable titles as "Making the MOOSt of It" and "MOOSt Unusual." She tends to focus on pop culture subject matter and relies heavily on man-on-the-street interviews for color commentary.

- CBS' STEVE HARTMAN:
  Hartman began with his belief that "Everybody Has a
  Story" and turned into a feature whereby he would toss
  a dart over his shoulder at a map of the United States.
  Wherever that dart landed is where he landed. Once
  there, he randomly opened the local phone book, pointed
  to a person, and told their story. The results were heartwarming, uplifting, surprising, unexpected, and had
  connectivity. Hartman went on with CBS with his "On the
  Road" and now "Kindness 101" segments. If you need a
  textbook lesson in crafting unique and powerful storytelling, I suggest you check out these two reporters...again
  and again.

  Many local market stations don't have the budgets for
  such specialized reporting but don't give up. They are a
  viewer favorite. Even the Fort Myers Florida NBC affiliate, which is budget-conscious market 54, has a reporter
  named Sean Martinelli who hosts the signature Emmy
  Award-winning Story2Share franchise which, much like
  Steve Hartman, features unique and emotional human-
  interest stories from Southwest Florida.

SO...TAKE MATTERS INTO YOUR OWN HANDS
If you want and can create these kinds of storytelling segments,
have a voice, and need an outlet; I suggest a YouTube channel. It is
a legitimate way to hone your skills and creates a catalog of stories/
segments for others to view. These days you can create stories using
your smartphone. Give it a try. You never know who is watching.
(We will discuss the potential of social media in a later section of this
book.) And you can direct potential employers to your YouTube channel as a form of on-screen audition. But remember, smart reporting
begins with smart writing. You want your story to have a beginning, a

middle, and an end. What is the premise? What is the subject matter? What are you trying to say? What is the outcome? Think about these issues before you set up the camera, even with an outline. It makes the job much easier.

I, TOO, HAVE BEEN THERE...
When I was first starting as a producer, I was encouraged from the very beginning to be in front of the camera. I took it as a compliment and just placed it in the back of my mind. That is until an opportunity arose while I was working at the Fox affiliate in Los Angeles. They were looking for a weekend weatherman and one of the reporters insisted I put together a tape and go for the job. I knew nothing about forecasting the weather, but she was undaunted by that obstacle. So, I created a voice of the "wacky weatherman"—a non-traditional segment whereby I wouldn't do it from the weather desk but rather from the field.

The segment I put together was at the beach where I had the lifeguard throw me a beach towel that, when I spread it out, had the temperatures spelled out on it. I did my extended forecast wading in the waves and walked around asking the beachgoers which was hotter: the temperature or...me? I went back to the station and edited a tight 3 minutes and gave it to my reporter friend who loved it. I told her my next segment was going to be on the Hollywood Walk of Fame where the temperatures were lined up on the famous stars on the sidewalk and I would ask the tourists what the weather was like back home. She again loved it. She took the tape to the news director.

The bottom line was I didn't become "The Wacky Weatherman", despite the positive review of the taped segment. But that tape did get me a reporter job at E! and the E! job got me a gig on EXTRA...and so on. Find your voice.

- COMPANIES THAT HAVE A SIGNIFICANT PRESENCE ON
  THE INTERNET
  While many companies on the internet are primarily fed with
  written stories, some also use video-driven segments as well.
  There are opportunities to make your mark as a reporter on
  the internet, but the same expectations of professionalism apply. Check out these sites to get an idea of how they work:

  - HUFFINGTON POST

  - 19TH NEWS

  - BUZZFEED

  - TMZ

  - CNET

" AND THEN THERE IS THE "L" WORD...LUCK!

I got lucky. Robin Williams discovered me. Not during an audition. Not at a comedy club. Not at a cocktail party, dinner party, social event, or through a friend...or even a friend of a friend. He picked me out on a red-carpet line to humiliate me and the rest was show biz history. I was a made man. We were in the development stages of the syndicated entertainment series EXTRA at the time. The management team wanted to create a new and different way to approach red-carpet events. I had been lured over and convinced to not sign a contract with E! Entertainment Television with the premise that I would be that red-carpet creative answer.

The opportunity presented itself by way of a type of audition of sorts. I was assigned to be on the carpet for the MTV Movie Awards. Now, by this stage in my career, I was a seasoned veteran of dozens of red-carpet events and had handled even more celebrity interviews, and I was aware of the handicap I was facing. EXTRA was yet to be on the air. There was simply no reason for a star to stop and talk to a microphone with no logo, for a segment on a show that wouldn't air, with a name that no one knew. Yet my career as a "clever red-carpet reporter" hinged on getting the stars and making them talk...and better yet, producing something different, more original, than that of stringing together a line of talking heads.

"Somewhere there is a curtain missing!" Robin Williams bellowed from halfway down the carpet and decidedly looked in my direction. To garner some sort of attention, I had chosen to wear a Versace-like bold patterned shirt that evening. It worked. As he approached, I instructed the cameraman to break the cardinal rule at the time and pull back to create a two-shot including both me and Williams in the ensuing interplay. The audience would need to see the shirt he was fixating on. "You couldn't decide on a color, so you picked them all," he ranted as he approached.

I gave as good as I got, not holding back but being self-deprecating to his one-liners. Up until that point, red carpet coverage was about the star arrivals. The reporter was non-existent as far as anything other than a facilitator of questions. This interplay redefined the way EXTRA would make red carpet coverage their own. Both ENTERTAINMENT TONIGHT and GOOD MORNING AMERICA had caught the happenings with Williams and played their versions of my dealings with the comedian on the carpet and I from that point on was "the shirt guy" on the red carpet.

 By the time we got on the air, I already had a comfortable relationship with stars and publicists alike, and my reporting career was sealed. People have said to me, having heard this anecdote, that I didn't have to pay my dues—that Robin Williams created a career for me. Dues are an interesting payment plan. What people don't take into consideration is that my years as a producer allowed me to think on my feet, realize an opportunity, adjust accordingly, and create the best possible segment out of the best-case scenario. The fact that I was rewarded for it is a win/win. But you can't tell me I didn't earn it.

PERSONALITY
ARE YOU TRYING TO CREATE AN "ACT?"

Perhaps you simply have a personality that shines; you're a natural-born showman. Perhaps you have created a "shtick" that needs a vehicle to be seen. Perhaps you do something extraordinary or popular and are looking to show the world. As long as you can wrap it in a personality-driven context, you are on to something. (Later in the SOCIAL MEDIA section of this book, we will explore how to create and use various media platform accounts to exploit your personality.)

Again, the internet and digital platforms are your friend. They are, for the most part, an unbridled opportunity to showcase what you have to offer. But I suggest:

- FIND A NICHE
  Are you funny? Great! How so? What do you do that can grab people's attention and keep it? Finding a niche and sticking to it is key to people gravitating to what you are offering. If you are all over the map, so too are the viewers—there will be no reason for them to return to your site, channel, Instagram, etc. if there is not a reasonable expectation to get more of what you do best. If you have even thought about getting into the process, then you know what you have to offer. Again:

    ◊ Set a goal as to what you want to achieve with getting into this process. Are your expectations realistic with what you have to offer?

    ◊ Make sure you have enough content to bank several episodes. You want viewers to follow you from the start, re-click, and know you will be there for their fleeting attention span.

◊ Practice what you are going to present. I like to use the comedian analogy of having a "tight three minutes"—meaning good and entertaining—rather than ten minutes that ramble on.

◊ The on-camera audience is different from a live audience. If there is something you need to emphasize for impact, do it. Pause ever so slightly if you think they will need time for information or content to sink in (somewhat like waiting for a laugh or holding for applause). But, overall, be clear in your delivery...you don't want the viewer to have to replay to understand because they won't.

- BE CONSISTENT

IN CONTENT
Does your niche have staying power from the start? If you are doing a parody of Stephen King novels, there are a lot of them, but the list is finite. So, there is a natural end. If you are doing a parody of scary novels, the list is endless. But, sticking with Steven King, should you do just his work and you become a sensation from what you create, you may not have to reach the end of his series to have achieved your desired goals.

IN TIME
If your normal segment is ninety seconds, give them ninety seconds regularly. If it is three minutes, give them three minutes. Viewers expect what they expect.

IN FREQUENCY
Post regularly...and preferably often...to maintain interest.

- DO IT WELL...BUT DON'T BE AFRAID TO BE IMPERFECT
  The viewer is not necessarily looking for what they find on traditional television when they search on the internet. They are looking for quirky and personality-driven content. If your product is slightly unpolished, amateurish, and looks home-made; that's fine. Post it anyway. Be considerate of your audience by following the previously mentioned suggestions and indicators, but don't lose the personality aspect of what you are bringing forth in the process. That is what you are selling.

  There are millions of popular and some still unfound personalities all over the internet. The following are three examples of personalities who brought a unique product to the internet space. Check out what they did, and analyze why their niche made them a success.

  - ◊ DAVEY WAVEY
    What did he do to make himself famous? Gay Guru. Okay...but he has had almost one hundred million views.

  - ◊ COLLEEN MAE BALLINGER a.k.a. MIRANDA SINGS
    What did she do to make herself famous? Comedian, actress, and singer who turned her alter-ego character satirizing people using YouTube to break into show business into a Netflix television series.

  - ◊ PEWDIEPIE
    What did he do to make himself famous? Played video games and commented on the experience. Now has upwards of thirty million followers on YouTube.

SELF PROMOTER

There is nothing wrong with self-promotion. And, I dare say, "gratuitous" is no longer a dirty word. The internet has created a cottage industry for the exploitation of traditional and non-traditional skill sets. Why not take advantage? If you can turn that into everything from a career alternative to a side hustle, I say go for it. But like anything, it takes work and commitment. The self-promoter falls into two categories:

INFLUENCER

While we will go into the subject matter of influencers in detail in the SOCIAL MEDIA section of this book, it is important to make note of defining points:

WHAT IS AN INFLUENCER?

An Influencer is a popular or authority figure within an industry who shares opinions, knowledge, or advice. If you can think of it, you can be an influencer. But that doesn't mean you will gather followers or viewers...or spread influence. It takes work to find your niche, consistency of content to gather a following, and personality and knowledge to keep interested.

THE DIFFERENT TYPES
Promotion is the principal idea behind influencing—either self (a skill, talent, trade, or advice) or a product.

NOT EVERYONE CAN BE A KARDASHIAN...
BUT NO ONE CAN BE YOU
The immense popularity of certain celebrity influencers should not daunt you. Your contribution is uniquely your own. It is up to you to create and build your site to maximize its full potential.

DO YOU HAVE SOMETHING TO SAY
It is as simple as having an interest, opinion, knowledge, and consistent content.

LESS IS MORE—DO ONE THING RIGHT
Specialize: If your expertise is shoes, do not talk about ice cream. Similarly, if your expertise is 'pop culture' and a shoe is all the rage one day, and an ice cream another then covers the spectrum under your greater umbrella. Remember you don't have to be an expert, but you do have to be creditable.

Credibility is a combination of knowledge and experience—knowing the subject matter and having "been there, done that." Why should anyone listen to you, or engage with you, if you can't speak eloquently about the subject matter? People, the viewer, the audience, the follower—their time matters. You have one shot at proving you are not wasting it.

HOW TO BECOME AN INFLUENCER?
The hard part is becoming an influencer; it is the maintaining and growth of your site where the real work deems you an influencer. Still, you have to start, and the following is where it all begins:

1. FIND A NICHE AND DEVELOP A CONTENT STRATEGY
    What is your expertise? Define it clearly and make the viewer/follower want more. Make sure you can create enough content to keep viewers clicking on and looking for more. Fans have a low attention span and will move on.

- **CHOOSE YOUR MEDIA PLATFORM**
  Where will you get the most exposure? TikTok,
  YouTube, Instagram...how about maintaining a
  presence on all platforms you can. It is essential.

2. **MAINTAIN A WEBSITE**
   Create a website that can be a hub for all your information
   and direct followers to your different platforms. You don't
   have to hire a website company and spend thousands of
   dollars to do this. Simple drag-and-drop do-it-yourself
   web portals such as WIX will walk you through the process.

   - **CREATE AN ENGAGING BIO—IMPRESS ME**
     Who are you? Why should we listen to/watch
     you? This is your chance to impress your audi-
     ence. List interesting facts about yourself, why
     you are interested in the subject matter you
     are purported to be an influencer on, and some
     educational, work, life, or expertise experience.

3. **ENGAGE WITH YOUR AUDIENCE AND BE CONSISTENT**
   Talk back with your viewers. Respond to their feedback.
   Answer their questions. Be consistent with your posts.
   Your viewers will be loyal to you if you are loyal to them.

4. **GROW YOUR NETWORK AND TRACK YOUR PROGRESS**
   You need to follow the business end of this process.

   - **UNDERSTAND YOUR AUDIENCE**
     Learn who your audience is to pinpoint demo-
     graphics that appeal to brand collaboration.

- ENGAGE BRANDS TO COLLABORATE
  Brands will come looking if you have what they need in terms of marketing value for their products.

- STAY CURRENT, UP TO DATE, AND HAVE A STRONG OPINION
  Follow the trends, develop opinions and comments based on facts, not rumors, and be current with information.

TEACHER/INSTRUCTOR/SKILL PROMOTER

Are you simply taking to the airwaves because you have a specific skill you wish to publicize or popularize? The internet is a good home for you. If you are demonstrating a skill—such as a chef who is promoting a cookbook—or instructing a task—such as video editing—or doing online teaching—such as conducting a yoga class; the organization is key:

KNOW THE NUMBER OF STEPS YOUR TASK WILL TAKE

Count the steps of the process. Make sure you cover everything as the audience is seeing this for the first time. Break down those steps into easy visuals.

BE CLEAR AND CONCISE IN YOUR EXPLANATION

Explain everything clearly. Just like with the number of steps, you are explaining to an audience who has never heard the instructions before. You need to be clear and simplified, even if you think it is too simple. But there is a difference between being simple and clear and talking down to your viewer. Keep your energy high and remember to talk to the viewer and not at the viewer. You may want to practice several times before committing to recording.

◊   MAKE SURE THE VISUALS MATCH THE TASK
Make sure what we are seeing is an example of what
you are saying. Do not jump ahead, or go backward.
You may want to record once for visuals, once with an
explanation, and once together and edit the finished
product together to make sure you have covered all
bases.

◊   CAN YOU CONDENSE THE TIME
Is this a long explanation? Or, does the process take
time? Does something you are building need time
to set or does a recipe need time to cook? If so you
may want to make more than one product and have
the finished piece ready to show rather than protract
production.

◊   IS THERE MORE THAN ONE EPISODE
Are you creating enough of a library of episodes to
keep the audience coming back?

COMMENTATOR

This section is not addressing the commentary-based shows as you
would see on the twenty-four-hour news channels. This is for those
with a voice and who want to express their opinion in a specific way
and find an audience.

WHAT IS A COMMENTATOR?

A commentator, by definition, is someone who possesses special skills
or knowledge to be credible and allowed to speak with authority
on a specific subject matter. These days, it seems like everyone has
something to say. But again, no one—at least those who establish
any amount of credibility—can speak on all things and all subjects.
Find your expertise and speak about what you know: sports, politics,

comedic observations, finances, etc. It is, as explained before, the equivalent of finding your niche.

HOW DO YOU GET ATTENTION?

KNOWLEDGE

Although it happens, I don't recommend a rambling speech on a subject matter you know nothing about—even if you have an opinion. Should you have an opinion or something to say:

- Do your research and back up your position with other facts, figures, or public perceptions that match your own.

  ◊ Be articulate. State your case with passion and en-thusiasm for sure, but make sure what you are saying makes sense. Even if people are going to disagree— and people will when it comes to commentary—pres-ent your position with a well-thought-out thesis that stands up for itself rather than a mixed jumble of thoughts strung together randomly. You will prove to be an effective speaker and well worth listening to.

PERSONALITY

You can be bombastic. You can be funny. You can be in your face. But you'd better be convincing. Your job is to make the audience feel that what you have to say is correct, grounded in fact, and is thought-driving or changing. Again, you can't be all things to all people. Find a comfortable presentation tone and persona and stick with it. Your likeability is almost as important as your content.

SOCIAL MEDIA

We will explore how social media works later in this book (Part 4), but you will want to exploit platforms like Twitter and Instagram to their fullest when it comes to opinion. Create a website that acts like a hub for all your activities and warehouses your segments as well. While you can transcribe your commentary for the printed page on your website, nothing gets your point across better than the visual of your speaking with passion and urgency.

WHAT IS THE POINT?

Only you can determine the end game in doing commentary because it can be incendiary at times depending on your point of view, delivery, and content or subject matter. But commentary can provide a wide range of opportunities for people that the definition in its current colloquial understanding doesn't always resonate. Such as:

♢   If you are a realtor, you could comment on the current state of the marketplace, interest rates, how to secure a mortgage, etc.

♢   If you are a lawyer, you could comment on easy-to-handle topics such as wills or setting up an LLC.

♢   If you are a comedian, you could do observational commentary in the style of Trevor Noah or Bill Maher and not just tell jokes.

♢   If you are a stockbroker, you could comment on financial advice.

The list goes on, but the bottom line is all of these commentaries are value-added to careers and boost the commentator to an expert level in their field.

ACTOR

It used to be when you were an actor, you were pigeonholed by the genre in which you worked: if you worked in movies you didn't work on television, if you worked on sitcoms you didn't work in dramas, and so on. Those days have, of course, ended. But many believed that if you started on a platform like YouTube, you never had a chance at the "Big Time!" But more and more, actors—from those aspiring to those established—are using internet platforms as a place of exposure for everything from resume reels to showcasing talent.

These are a few internet actors who have transferred to the large screen:

- GRACE HELBIG: Turning her DailyGrace 2.4 million subscribers into roles in TROLLS and THE WEDDING YEAR.

- JIMMY TATRO: Has turned his 3.4 million viewers of his self-produced comedy skits into roles in 22 JUMP STREET, AMERICAN VANDAL, MODERN FAMILY, and SMALLFOOT.

- ANNA AKANA: One half of a comedy music duo, she landed the ultimate prize in a hit franchise movie ANT-MAN.

- LILY SINGH: One of the highest-paid YouTubers with 14 million subscribers and billions of views worldwide, she has parlayed her fame into roles in BAD MOMS, THE BAD GUYS, F THE PROM, and DOLLFACE.

- FLULA BORG: Took on Hollywood via YouTube Germany to land a role in PITCH PERFECT 2. But that is just the beginning. He's no struggling actor with roles in high-profile projects like THE GOOD PLACE, RALPH BREAKS THE INTERNET, AQUAMAN: KING OF ATLANTIS, and THE SUICIDE SQUAD among others.

Have they done anything others can't? The simple answer is no. But to get a better perspective on the value of the alternative options for

today's actors, I have turned to two business colleagues who provided
their first advice:

SIDEBAR: KEVIN SPIRTAS

*30-year veteran Broadway, film, and television actor, KEVIN SPIR-
TAS, is best known for his long-running role as Dr. Craig Wesley on
the NBC daytime soap opera DAYS OF OUR LIVES. But recently, as
co-creator of the six-time EMMY Award-winning digital drama series
AFTER FOREVER (Spirtas, himself, winning for Lead Actor in a Digital
Drama, and along with his late co-creator Michael Slade, winning
Outstanding Digital Drama 2019, and Outstand Writing Team for
Digital Drama 2019 and 2020). That is quite an achievement for a
project that was self-developed, privately financed, independently
produced, and placed on, rather than sold to, a streaming service.*

So how did this all come about?

> *"I had moved to New York after my time on DAYS OF OUR
> LIVES had come to an end. And while no roles were com-
> ing my way that spoke to me or sang to me, I began ex-
> ploring what my friends were doing on digital platforms.
> They were creating personal content that was inspiring,
> touching, authentic, and real. It was better content than
> I was seeing on traditional television."*

> *"So, I thought to myself if I was to create content, what
> would it be? And I had to give it a lot of thought. I was,
> at that time, a single gay man of an age who wanted to
> find love. Would that make an interesting dating se-
> ries?"*

> *"I am not by past profession a creator but as luck would
> have it, I ran into a former colleague Michael Slade, a*

*writer from DAYS OF OUR LIVES, who was willing to listen
to my thoughts—which at its core was about gay men
who are not 30 anymore. He thought we should talk
more."*

*"Michael knew how to write, and I knew the ins and outs
of raising funds. It was the right match at the right time.
But we weren't quite sure what to do with the product.
We could have done a pilot, and attempted to sell it to a
production company and/or a network, but that would
have been the end of our participation in our project.
We decided to go for it. Raise the money and self-dis-
tribute, which you can do with YouTube, on a website,
or a platform like Amazon Prime. The budget was about
as much as an indie film; the entirety of season one was
filmed in ten days—8 episodes, 7-12 minutes a piece."*

*"Sure, there were challenges...not compromises, but
challenges. But as we entered into the worldwide film
festival circuit, and received award after award, capped
off by the EMMY acknowledgments, we knew it had
been worth keeping our vision and control, and integrity
intact. Going this route isn't easy to earn your money
back. You do earn money from viewership, sales, potential foreign syndication, and having the opportunity to
sell the format to foreign markets."*

*"My co-creator, co-executive producer, and true inspira-
tion, Michael Slade, passed away before we could go
into production on season three—the conclusion of this
trilogy story. And that was an immense blow to my
creative process, not to mention the personal loss. But
we, as a team, hope to have done him proud with this*

final series. Because, as much as I am empowered to do more...I know I never would have started in the first place without him."

Kevin's tips for anyone inspired by his story and looking to explore alternative platforms as a creative outlet:

- ◊ *DON'T LIMIT THE CREATIVE PROCESS OR CREATIVE PATH Your good idea is just that... GOOD...so work toward the best of your creative process and follow your most assertive creative path. But be prepared that the best ideas come together through teamwork. Keeping as much focus within that team is up to you.*

- ◊ *STORY IS EVERYTHING*
  A concept is just an idea. Have a solid story to tell. Think about how it is original, compelling, and authentic. On a bigger scale, does it have a place in the marketplace? Is it what is selling? There is nothing wrong with producing a 'labor of love' project...but it is even better to have a project that can return an investment.

- ◊ *DON'T BE AFRAID TO ASK FOR HELP*
  Whether it is financial or within the production process, you get nowhere without help. So look to people you trust and know their experience matches your needs.

- ◊ *COLLABORATION IS KEY*
  You may have a vision and even experience, but no one is an expert in all aspects of the

creative/production process. Rely upon the expertise of others. It will inevitably make you shine as well.

◊ **WHEN IT COMES TO FINANCING, FIND PEOPLE WHO MATCH THE CONTENT**
You want to be partnered with people who understand your content, and subject matter and want to buoy you up rather than take control.

SIDEBAR: JADE GENGA

Actress, choreographer, acting consultant, and author (THE ITTY BITTY GRITTY OF NEW YORK CITY—for Actors), JADE GENGA is a third-generation show business veteran. Granddaughter to recording artist, record producer, and music executive Gerry Granahan and actress Marylou Kiernan and daughter to actress and dancer Gerrianne Genga comes by her expertise honestly. Having grown up working her way in the industry "the way things used to be", she is still young enough to utilize today's new platforms to coach aspiring newcomers on how to exploit for maximum exposure.

How do you see the internet as a help?
"It took off to what it has become today as a result of two factors: the pandemic and the expense of living in the entertainment meccas, cities like New York, Chicago, Los Angeles, and Chicago. Life in the city was 90% survival and 10% hustle; so many of the struggling creative community moved away. But to stay active in the business, people posted on the internet—showcase performances, audition reels, etc. And the industry responded accordingly."

"So, a lot of talented people who never got a chance to

be 'in the room' have gotten a chance to show their stuff. Similarly, when you do get some attention on the internet, it is longer than thirty seconds and a 'next' shouted at you. The internet has, on so many levels, leveled the playing field."

"But it is a double-edged sword. The human aspect of an open audition is gone. Who you are when you walk into the room is lost. So what is happening now is that many auditions are asking for digital submissions first and a live call back second. But even asking for digital submissions has been somewhat overwhelming for casting directors, directors, and producers. I know of one recent call which received 7000 submissions versus the several hundred they would have normally encountered. That is simply too overwhelming. So, what do you do?"

"The key, from my perspective, is to have a well-curated audition reel. Yes, you can post additional segments and achievements and showcase a range of talent...but...it is key to network social media. Make connections, solicit references, and expand your circle. If you worked with thirty people in the repertory, stay in contact with them. You never know where they end up. One way 7000 submissions get weeded through is to check references. Yours will matter."

"So, while having one curated video for auditions is important, don't be afraid to showcase your personality in other segments. But, remember, several good show-case postings are far better than hundreds of postings of every pirouette you've ever spun or monologue you've ever uttered. Edit out the outdated, unnecessary, extra-

neous videos you don't believe will showcase you in the best possible light. Better yet, don't post them in the first place."

And that is a perfect segue to Jade's tips for any aspiring actor:

    ◊ ***SHOWCASE WHAT YOU WANT TO DO—NOT WHAT YOU THINK YOU HAVE TO DO***
Many people, certainly early in their careers, believe they have to be all things to all people. You don't and, most probably, you can't. You want to post your best you. Polish, then perform, then post.

    ◊ ***REMEMBER EVERYTHING ON THE INTERNET IS FOREVER***
Do not post what you do not want to come back and haunt you later. Think about your future career and the ability to have one. Whatever you are doing now may seem harmless, funny, or daring; but may cost you later on.

    ◊ ***IS YouTube THE NEW 8x10?***
No! You still need a good but personable 8x10. What do I mean by personable? Gone are the days when they are looking for those Hollywood-esque, staged, beauty shots. Today, they want to see you. It may be a little quirky, but it will catch their eye. Why is this important? Because when an open audition is called, the first thing a casting director will see is a thumbnail of your 8x10. If they don't click on it, they won't see your audition reel,

and so on. So, remember it is not about pearly whites...it's all about personality.

◊　**TAKE THE HIGH ROAD**
Because they are not facing you in person, people feel free to be armchair critics. They can be petty and very personal. Just let it go. You will face criticism your entire career. It is part of the job.

◊　**BE AUTHENTIC**
You are who you are and you do what you do. Only you do it. Own it. Don't try to be some-one else, take a page from someone else's act, or replicate someone else's video. Do you well...that is all anyone can ask.

PART THREE:

THE NUTS AND BOLTS OF HOW TELEVISION WORKS

This part of this book is about how to be on television, not how to make television. You may want to get a different book If you don't know how television works. There are plenty of textbooks out there that will explain in great detail how the camera works; how the angles affect the shot, the atmosphere, the storytelling; how the lighting is set up to effectively do the same thing; and how editing creates the finished result. And for those needs, I am going to suggest the following:

- The more technical: TELEVISION PRODUCTION HANDBOOK, 12TH EDITION by Herbert Zettl
- The more user friendly: HOW TO SHOOT VIDEO THAT DOESN'T SUCK by Steve Stockman

Fortunately, today, the internet is also full of tutorials on how your camera works and editing is learned. But most devices are extremely user-friendly and even the most amateur amongst us can make broadcast quality content in no time.

WHAT IS TV THESE DAYS?

I often hear, "I don't watch TV." Yet that same person is well aware and has seen the latest and talked about trending programming. But because they didn't watch it on a "cable" or "traditional" network, and because they watched it on an iPad, they didn't believe they had watched television. As we discussed, television does not have to be on a televise set or watched on the flat screen in the family living room anymore.

- DIFFERENT DEVICES
  From traditional sets to tablets to computers, and telephones, the content—no matter what the device—is still considered "tele"-vision. You can now download apps from networks, streaming, and the internet to any device and watch effort-lessly. This is why, if you choose to create your channel, you too are creating "television."

  - PLATFORMS

    - NETWORKS
      These are considered the stalwart traditional founding networks of television: ABC, NBC, CBS, and later FOX. Their programming style and phi-losophy have remained relatively the same over the decades.

    - CABLE
      When cable came along, the bandwidth of televi-sion increased to hundreds of channels. While HBO and Mtv were founding cable networks of the early days and fell into niche broadcasting, cable networks today jockey for popularity and stretch the range of programming to do so. You may come to know one or another for the type of programming they offer but more and more, headline-grabbing programming is important to lure the viewer within a saturated marketplace.

    - STREAMING
      Netflix, Hulu, Amazon Prime, and Apple TV are examples of these subscription-based networks which don't require your attachment to tradi-tional television broadcasters to take advantage of, there are tier rates of pricing to pay for the various services they offer—mostly do you want to advertise or not? These networks allow you to

watch programming on demand and coined the
notion of "binge-worthy" series—short, 6-10 episode series, that viewers will watch in one sitting.

- INTERNET
YouTube is the most obvious example of television
on the internet. Although, companies like Meta,
the parent company of Facebook are aggressively
moving in on the territory.

What is a YouTube channel? A YouTube channel
is a personal portal available to anyone who joins
YouTube as a member. You can have more than
one channel and you can have a personal channel
as well as a business channel. Both will allow you
to upload videos. (We will explore the value of a
YouTube channel later on in the Social Media section, Part 4 of this book.)

Suffice it to say, with billions of users, worldwide,
YouTube is a formidable entertainment vehicle.

CAMERA EQUIPMENT

DIFFERENT KINDS OF CAMERAS

Cameras are, quite frankly, a personal choice. Only you can decide
what your needs are and how sophisticated a setup with which you
are looking to equip yourself. The following are the three camera options you can expect to work with:

- DSLR

- CAMCORDERS

- GO PRO

In terms of brands, Canon consistently ranks high, with several models making top ten lists. But your brand loyalty to say, Sony or Nikon, may make you more comfortable with their products. You have to look at the price—assuming you can start at just under $1000 for a camera outfit and go on to many thousands for more sophisticated equipment—or decide by features that will dictate both brand and price.

One thing to consider with your camera choice is what you intend to do with it and whether will require additional equipment. Will that equipment need to interface with that camera? Such as using external microphones. Does the camera have an input for that? How big of a tripod do you need? Your camera package must accommodate both your immediate and future needs. So think ahead. Think big picture.

- CELL PHONE
  Fortunately, your smartphone is equipped with a rather sophisticated camera already.   The phone has a built-in light, microphone, and stabilizer. Broadcast-quality television commercials and even feature films have been shot with iPhones. The smartphone has come a long way. Use it.

  Given that a smartphone has its obvious limitations, the industry has created a plethora of accessories to make the production process more professional. For the more advanced user, you will want to invest in accessories made specifically for the YouTube/Vlog community. Look into these options:

    - Selfie tripod/mount rig

    - Ring light/shotgun lights

    - External directional microphone/Lavalier microphones

LIGHTING

Let's take a moment to take note of lighting as lighting can make or break your video. The viewer will notice the impact of good or correct lighting. Creative lighting can establish a mood, manipulate the time of day, pinpoint information or details, create an alternative reality, and establish three dimensions. Something as simple as a ring light surrounding your smartphone makes all the difference in the recording quality you make for YouTube. If you aspire to be a makeup influencer, for instance, you want that ring light to show your face in the best possible light. You get the idea. Close-up lighting is just one aspect. Lighting subject matter requires understanding the basics of lighting techniques.

The basic canon for designing a workable lighting design is called 3-point lighting. 3-point lighting uses three light sources to illuminate the subject matter, providing basic shape, three dimensions, and separating the subject from the background. These three light sources are the KEY, FILL, and BACK lights.

- KEY light: This is the dominant light source focusing on the subject—say an interview. Typically, the key light is at least twice as bright as the side-fill light. In the typical 3-point design, the KEY light is placed 45 degrees to the subject's side, and at a 45-degree angle above the subject.

- FILL light: This is placed on the opposite side of the interview or subject matter and at approximately the same height and angle as the key light.   But usually, the fill light is at least half as bright as the key light. This provides a dimension to the shading of the subject matter, rather than a harsh flat face on lighting design.

- BACK light: This is placed behind the subject, again at about a 45-degree angle above and behind the subject. The brightness

of the backlight can range in intensity from the level of the fill
light to that of the key light, depending on the reflectivity of
your subject—what are they wearing, is the subject dark or
light, shiny or dull?

In combination, these lights provide basic illumination of the subject.
By manipulating the brightness of the key and fill lights shadowing is
created which gives the illusion of 3 dimensions to the subject. The
backlight then helps define the subject's shape and separates it from
the background.

You should explore an investment in a lighting kit when you are looking at your equipment budget.

EDITING

Again, if you are looking for a primer that will teach you how to edit
your content into a finished content segment, you have picked up the
wrong book. There are plenty of tutorials on the web that will teach
you the steps from basic to advanced. But I suggest that having even
basic editing skills are value added in today's marketplace. Many
news reporters, especially in smaller television markets, are expected
to shoot and edit their segments as well as appear on camera. But
creating captivating, entertaining, attractive content doesn't happen
on the fly. It is only enhanced by clever editing. No one expects you
to be the next Steven Spielberg but a little creative contouring can
only help.
Editing doesn't have to cost you a fortune. The following is a list of
the top five free editing programs available:

1. iMovie
    This is only for Mac users. It is for the beginner editor but is
    extremely user-friendly. The downside is that it has limited
    effects and only two channels of video.

2. OPENSHOT

   It runs on Mac and Windows and is excellent for beginners. It
   has a reasonable number of effects but is a little clunky and
   can run slowly.

3. VN VIDEO EDITOR

   This is run on an app and on Mac whereby you can start editing on the go on the app and airdrop the project to your computer and finish it there. There are a lot of effects.

4. KDENLIVE

   This is more suited to the intermediate-level editor. This
   would be a more professional-level version than Openshot.

5. DAVINCI RESOLVE

   This would be considered professional-level editing. It requires a newer computer with an updated operating system to
   handle its capacity.

The following are the best of the payment systems:

1. FINAL CUT PRO

   Can edit 8k video. Has a $300 cost but has a 90-day free trial.

2. CYBERLINK POWERDIRECTOR 365

   This features 3000 effects, edits 8k video, and has access to 6
   million stock photos and music.

3. ADOBE PREMIER PRO

   Can edit 8k and VR content. Is the most highly rated system,
   but is the most expensive at $55 a month which includes After
   Effects technology.

YOUR LOOK

Defining how you look on camera is key. Lady Gaga and Madonna may have made a career out of reinventing themselves, but I don't suggest it. Knowing what works for you and sticking with it may be playing it safe but when starting …it is better to be safe than sorry. Having said that, you don't have to be boring, just consistent. If your look happens to be bold colors or patterns and that works for what you are trying to achieve, then go for it. Just don't fall into the trap of appearing over the top when the content you are presenting trends to the conservative.

So, what works for you?

CAMERA ANGLES

Michael J Fox once told me all about his signature look—a ¾ glance with a slight tilt down and a semi-smile. He knew his good side. And he popped into the look in an instant. He said he perfected it so that a picture would never go bad. Smart. The lesson learned: know your camera angles.

- We all have a good…or at least a better side to our face. To know yours, stand in front of the bathroom mirror and place a hand mirror down the middle of your face highlighting one or the other side. Make a note of what you see and then reverse the process. You will inevitably like one side more than the other. That is the side you want to favor in pictures.

- When it comes to using your cell phone or doing any head and shoulder interview for that matter, the more desirable angle is to place the camera slightly higher above you. I emphasize slightly so that you elongate your neck. Lower camera angles force you to look down and can create double chins and large nostril shots. Both unflattering looks.

- When it comes to shooting yourself, or any subject matter, try not to center the person. Keeping the person slightly off-center is much more interesting framing.

- Lastly, don't be afraid to play—especially if you are creating for the internet. Stimulating and creative content is far more entertaining and likely to get views than staid traditional segments. I suggest trying several different options before settling on one definitive look.

GENERAL APPEARANCE

LEARN TO DO YOUR OWN MAKE-UP

Men, this applies to you too! No two make-up artists, no two camera setups are the same, and no two studios or settings are the same. Learn to know what your look is and know how to create it—and I am not talking about a quick coating of powder. It is worth investing in a good make-up training session and buying the suitable materials. This is essential as you don't want to look washed out under today's sophisticated lighting. Looking vibrant and healthy is important. You don't want to distract the viewer.

CLOTHES MAKE THE PERSON

Do you have a look? You can run the gamut but it should work for your message, personality, and subject matter. Be consistent with that look as it compliments your credibility.

BE TRUE TO YOUR BRAND
There is an old expression: clothes make the man. I will go further and say that clothes make the brand—and you are the brand you are trying to sell. Packaging any product is an integral part of marketing. Think of your look as packaging. You want the packaging to complement, help deliver the message subliminally and literally, and define a consistency of presence. Ask yourself:

- Are you formal?

- Are you informal?
  Does that mean prep school chic, sporty, or haute couture?

When you can define your brand and match it with a look remember there is always room for some cross-pollinating.

To be effective in changing up your look of your brand, rely on being consistent with making sure the look matches the message:

FOR MEN:
A suit and tie say authority but so can solid colors if a suit and tie are not right for a particular setting. But feel free to pick non-traditional suits such as windowpane fabrics rather than a simple blue suit if you wish to evoke a younger point of view. But, having to defer to a staid and formal message or brand is no excuse not to have a well-tailored, stylized suit along with which you can make a bold statement with a colorful or patterned tie.

Why can jeans and a black turtleneck be so effective a

look? Neutrality. Pair that with a black sports jacket and you've amped up the package. You could make the statement bolder with loafer shoes and no socks. All together you exude casual chic confidence. There is no distraction from the message and the delivery. You can say anything with credibility if you choose a neutral palette.

FOR WOMEN:
Women have far more choices facing them. Consistency is the key. Pick a look, a style, a designer, a fabric, color palette that works and stick with it. Hillary Clinton, for instance, stays with pant suits and no handbags. I would recommend staying away from loud patterns UNLESS that is a gimmick or statement you are trying to make specifically. And defer to classic dressing rather than trends. Simple is sometimes smarter and less distracting than giving the audience something to critique.

An easy way to be consistent:
I did a documentary series that was going to require several weeks of travel and outfits from casual daywear to evening casual. My answer was to buy color coordinates—sweaters, dress shirts, t-shirts, and polo shirts all from the same manufacturer in the same color. I bought several neutral colors. And in that way, no matter what situation I found myself in, I would be consistently dressed and not jarring the viewer from outfit to outfit.

Alternately, I have also used clothes as a signature. As I explained my relationship with Robin Williams, he tweaked to my loud shirt. The show and I thought it would be fun to keep me in loud shirts as a gimmick. It worked. Can you incorporate a look to add value to what you are doing...but not distract? The late Steve Jobs did it brilliantly with his familiar black turtleneck tops and jeans.

PART FOUR:

WHO ARE YOU?

Creating a persona is as important as creating a subject matter niche. A hard news reporter may have very little leeway other than to emote an authoritative personality but a niche reporter or internet personality can
be defined by their character.

DEFINING A PERSONALITY

While you must remain factual with your content, your delivery will shape viewer trust, credibility, and popularity. Do not create a false character but rather a persona that fits the subject matter.

The following are characteristics that can define a personality:

1. HONESTY
    First and foremost, it is all about facts and truth. You don't want to 'create' facts to fit the narrative. You can't suppose or insinuate. You must know what you are talking about. There are always legal issues to consider and you never want to find yourself behind a slander or libel suit. Moreover, the audience will always see through the disingenuous personality.

2. CLARITY
    Be clear in your delivery. Whether it is facts, commentary, or comedy; you do not want to race through the content and lose the audience. Enunciate, take your time and deliver to the audience even though you can't see them. Remember to talk to your viewer, not at them. There is a difference.

And don't talk down to them. You may be trying to tell them information but inform them don't pontificate—yours is not a sermon.

3. DO YOU HAVE PASSION/GENUINE INTEREST/ CURIOSITY?

One type of persona is a personality with a curiosity for the subject matter. You explore along with the viewer. Show your passion and interest and express it, so that the viewer follows along with the vicarious adventure.

4. EXPERTISE

Are you an expert such as astronomer Neil Degrasse Tyson or scientist Bill Nye the Science Guy or any one of the plethora of chefs or home decorators out there itching to show your skills? Well, from the internet to traditional television there are places for you. The secret to your success is a niche that sets you apart from others and a valued and unique expertise people are looking for. Once you have established that, it is about delivery and personality. What makes your information and expertise compelling and, even more importantly, enter-taining? The bottom line is: why should I watch...YOU? What are you telling me that grabs me and how are you telling it to me that makes me want to watch?

Here are three examples of expert personalities and why they work:

- Chip and Joanna Gaines from the Magnolia Net-work. Their folksy personalities—his "goofy" and hers the "every mom"—bely their crafty expertise. They work off each other in a joking sort of way only to come together to get the job done. They are part family sitcom and part 'do-it-yourself', and all expertise.

- Drew and Jonathan Scott—the Property Broth-ers—are identical twin home renovators who don't necessarily finish each other's sentences as they do finish each other's ideas. They are stylish without being obnoxious and work in harmony to bring out the best in each other proving the whole is greater than the sum of its parts.

- Martha Stewart. The bottom line with Martha is no matter how simple or intricate, whether it is in the kitchen, crafting, or in the garden; the experience is elevated. She makes you feel like you have done something of quality or fur-thered your living experience. It is a vicarious adventure for the viewer in the DIY "LIFESTYLES OF THE RICH AND FAMOUS" genre.

5. FISH OUT OF WATER

This personality is the viewer on television. You are going through the process of exploration with the viewer, uncover-ing as you go. You have to have an extreme curiosity, willing to try new things, and be quick to ask the questions that the viewer inevitably needs to know. The late Daniel Bourdain in the series PARTS UNKNOWN was a savvy explorer in this niche. And Stanley Tucci in his series SEARCHING FOR ITALY plays a similar role.

A COUPLE OF OBSERVATIONS FROM MARC FREDEN

THE POWER OF WALKING IT BACK:
SHOW YOUR VULNERABILITY

As an entertainment reporter, I learned that the 'entertainment' factor in my segments was key. But not everyone got the joke. When creating a brand or finding a niche, there will be some segments that work and others that will inevitably fall flat. You will learn from those. But try to create a failsafe if there is a person/subject who is part of the segment by which, if you feel things are going well, you can find an easy way to pivot the segment away from the awkward moment. Plan for this. Because, as I said, not everyone will get the joke.

There is a fine line between being funny or entertaining, and being offensive. At that point, my go-to was self-deprecation. I turned the joke back on me. What I suggest is you always make sure you are aware when you are pushing the envelope and you don't turn off or shut down your subject person. Being too familiar is a fine line to walk but creating a comfortable space for them gets the most out of them. When things are seeming a little tense, walk it back and take the responsibility to perform off the subject and go a little more mainstream.

" YOU GOTTA HAVE A GIMMICK...

I always had a gimmick for every entertainment event I covered. I once had to cover a red-carpet event that had a famous meal to follow. The media was not allowed into the meal part of the event...but that was the real emphasis of the event. So, what could I do to make this story interesting without access? This is what I did. As the stars arrived, I handed out doggie bags and asked them to bring me a little something from their plate as I would not be able to enjoy the meal. They thought that was hysterical and sure enough, the celebrities started sneaking out with bags of food for me with descriptions of the event inside. It made for a great segment. "

Obviously, in hard news, there is no room for comedy, but in lifestyles, niche broadcasting doesn't be afraid to look human. Show your mistakes. Rachel Ray does that all the time and is still engaging as a host and chef. We are not perfect people. Do not expect to be perfect on camera. You can be more engaging if you are less perfect and buttoned down.

THE POWER OF THE TWO SHOT

I have already shared my story of Robin Williams on the red carpet, pulling back to the two-shot, to record the banter between us. The two shot is key on many occasions. The interplay between you and your subject matter gives valuable credibility. Yes, this is now a world of Zoom interviews, but while you may have no option, an in-person interview is always preferable. Why? Reading body language—theirs and yours—makes a big difference in the quality of the content.

WHAT ARE YOU TRYING TO SAY?

This is an important question. You should think about not just what you are saying but why you are trying to say it. This will certainly direct your message to the audience you are trying to reach if you know your motivation.

IS THERE A MESSAGE OR DO YOU JUST WANT TO BE HEARD? You simply may just have an opinion or a series of opinions you wish to get out to an audience. That is fine. That doesn't mean you do not have to adhere to the aforementioned points of performance to gain the most viewers. But a message or commentary can be different from an opinion.

- Message: This may have the information necessary for public safety or updates for events for example. This must be factually correct.

- Commentary: How does this differ from opinion? I define opinion as "I don't like what this person is wearing." Whereas the commentary is taking an issue and expounding on the merits as you agree or disagree with them. This is a matter of interpreting the facts.

- In either case, the words matter. Don't shoot from the hip. Be aware of the context of your content and stay on point. That doesn't mean you can't be colorful and clever...just be correct.

ARE YOU SPEAKING FOR YOURSELF OR OTHERS?
Speaking for yourself is much easier as you own your words, opinions, commentary, and content in general. When speaking for others, you must be careful not to misrepresent the other person's thoughts, intent, or context.

PART FIVE:

HOW TOs AND BASIC UNDERSTANDINGs

This segment is designed to hone your skills and remind you of what you need to think about as you create distinctive, innovative, creative, informative, or entertaining work. The following emphasizes your strengths creatively rather than technically but both are necessary to create successful programming.

FOCUS

You can't be all things—think of the phrase "jack of all trades, master of none." You will need to narrow your focus, and create a niche that ensures enough subject matter to sustain a library of content. This is especially important if you are creating a YouTube channel or similar individual broadcast content subject matter.

These are my five tips to keep you on focus:

1. KEEP YOUR NICHE NARROW BUT DIVERSE

    a. Think of a box of Crayola Crayons. They are all crayons, that is the subject, but they are all different colors. And therein lies the diversity.

    b. Let's say you have a skill such as cooking videos. Stick with a specialty.

        i. CAN DO: DESERTS, MAIN COURSES, AND AP-PETIZERS

        ii. CAN'T DO: ITALIAN, CHINESE, AND GREEK (Unless your specialty is international cooking... don't be all over the map—pun intended.)

2. BUILD A REPERTORY OF SEVERAL SEGMENTS
Before you even start on the air, have several segments produced so that viewers can click on and follow you instantly, and not have to wait for additional products. Viewers'/followers' attention span is limited. You want to capture them and keep them.

3. LESS IS MORE
We will explore this later but don't babble, ramble or otherwise drag out a segment. It is better to be concise (think about a comedian having a "tight three minutes" rather than a monologue) rather than protracted and boring.

4. CHECK YOUR EXPECTATIONS
You will not be a star overnight. Even viral video takes time to register.

5. LISTEN TO FEEDBACK...ENCOURAGE FEEDBACK
Feedback is your friend. You can learn a lot about your connectivity with your audience through their feedback. If your goal is to be an influencer, this is critical. Even reporters on traditional television outlets no longer survive without a social media connection these days through which feedback and interaction are encouraged. From your on-air look to your comments, opinions, ability to deliver information and likeability is all fair game. Get ready to take it...and don't be defensive. Remember, you are a product...it is not personal.

DEVELOP INTERVIEW SKILLS

We will talk in-depth about how to face an interview in the PUBLIC SPEAKING segment of the book. But until then, consider the following:

An interview is a skill set. It is not simply asking a series of questions. You have an agenda to fulfill. You inevitably have a story to
tell, and that interview or series of interviews allows you to make that
story come alive with a beginning, middle, and end. Your interview
should also have a bit of a story arc to it as well. You usually have a
set amount of time or maybe an allotted number of questions you can
ask. Keep these three primary rules in mind:

- Make sure you cover as much territory as you can.
- Don't repeat questions or covered subject matter.
- Be persistent and do not settle for evasive answers.

AND... DO NOT ASK YES OR NO QUESTIONS

I shouldn't have to tell you this but even the best of us will fall into
this trap. Sometimes the essence of the question is just necessary.
But that doesn't mean you can't find a cleverer way to ferret out the
information you need rather than being stopped short with a yes or
no. If you have a yes or no question, the better way to approach it is
to ask: "Why?" For example: Do not ask: "Do you like ice cream?
Ask: "Why do you like ice cream?" Or, if you want to be even more
clever, ramp it up by asking: "What is it about ice cream that you find
so enjoyable?"

IT ISN'T JUST ABOUT THE QUESTION...

LISTEN TO THE ANSWER.

It is as simple as that. Listening is important. It is one thing to prepare notes and have an agenda for your interview, and I encourage
you to do your research (we will discuss this later), but you can't be
too ridged not to pivot if you hear valued information that takes you
in new and unexpected directions.
Listening should:

- Take you in a new and different direction than your interview was initially heading. Be careful that the direction doesn't make you stray off course.

- Remind the interviewee that you are interested in what they are saying. This is important with engagement. You get more out of them if the interviewee feels you are part of the conversation and not just going down a list of questions.

- Allow you to learn something. You may get new information that teaches you valuable lessons. You want to be prepared that you are interviewing the expert, but you are not the expert.

On a personal note: I don't believe in having notes in front of me when I am conducting an interview. Notes tell the interviewee that I have an agenda and might not fully engage in what they are saying. Not having notes allows for a more conversational approach. And not having notes gives me the freedom to connect with more eye contact and not look down and break the flow. It is a skill to keep your questions and agenda in your head but it is well worth the effort for the results you get.

- DRIVE THE CAR:
  Remember, you are in control of the interview. You know what you need from the interviewee and in what direction the interview needs to go. But the interviewee isn't always on board with that. Their answers may take you in a different direction. Again, listen to see if the car is drifting into a new lane. You are driving the car. You cannot insult your interview subject by saying something such as: "We're not here to talk about that…" But you can say something like: "That is a very interesting observation, but what do you think about this…"

My personal style of interviewing is very conversational and that
has left me vulnerable for give-and-take dialogue. Remember, I
am not the subject of the interview. So, if I am asked a question,
which I can't disregard to not appear to be rude and dismissive, I
am eating up a precious allotted interview time. It is up to me to
stare my answer back to a question to move the interview along.

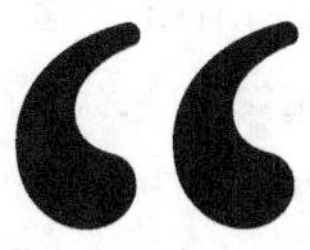

BARBRA STEISAND...GETTING HIGH

**I had this very problem with Barbra Streisand during
a half-hour interview to promote her album HIGHER
GROUND. We were in the middle of discussing one thing or another and she mentioned how she related to the late Princess Diana
in that she too was hounded by paparazzi and asked me what I
thought of that whole situation. That question had nothing to do
with the album, would not be part of the finished segment, and was
very deep and, if I answered, would eat up a lot of the time we had
left. I simply said that the situation was complicated and asked her
if she thought she could make a difference by speaking out. She said
she could. And I suggested that perhaps that was her
moving to HIGHER GROUND. And we were back on
track talking about the album. See what I did there?**

BODY LANGUAGE

Body language is key when conducting an interview. Think about
it. What would you think about a person who is slouching, head
down, and can't make eye contact? Would you take them seriously
or believe that they are interested in the conversation you are about
to have? An interview is a conversation...BE PRESENT at the moment.
Part of driving the car is the subtle message of body language. It
starts with a good posture that shows you are both respectful but also
engaged. But there are a few tricks that you can use to get even the
most reluctant interviewee to succumb to more emotive answers.

I was a producer on an NBC daytime show called LOVE STORIES. The premise was simple: There were two couples. Both had fallen in love most dramatically and both had broken up most spectacularly. But only one got back together. The audience had to guess which couple got back together.

The entire show was done in a "he said/she said" continuous interview format—no narration. If the producer didn't get the details, they didn't exist. The problem was if they were the couple who broke up for good, it was hard for them to talk in loving terms about how they fell in love and the same was for the opposite.

These body language interview tricks proved not only invaluable to making that show work but proved handy for interviewing in all aspects of other interview circumstances:

- FACIAL EXPRESSIONS
  If you need your subject matter to smile, then smile at them. If you need them to be sad, put on a sad face. It is like yawning; your facial expressions are infectious. Try to emote what you would like your interviewee to emote.

- PREGNANT PAUSE
  If the interviewee is at a point of contemplation...DON'T SPEAK. Let them go through the process of emotion. They may begin to laugh or cry but the moment will be lost if you take them out of it. People are nervous about silence. They will fill it. And chances are they will fill the silence with something you want to hear or see.

- WHISPER
  Softening your voice makes the interviewee do one of two things or both. One, lean in to hear you which, is perceived that you have said something that is relevant and that they

want to express the importance. Second, they, too, lower
their voice which expresses empathy, sadness, or the revealing
of information. Doing both makes the viewer feel that they
have just leaned in to let them know something valuable is
about to be told.

- LEAN IN
  If you lean in, many times so will they. Again, the lean-in expresses that they have something important to say.

DO YOUR RESEARCH

Do not go into an interview blind. You want to know the thrust of
where the interview is going to go. If you are tossed a curveball
during the interview or you are being deceived, you need to know it
is happening. You aren't going to know that if you haven't done at
least the basics of research. The other advantage is that you might be
surprised by the information that is completely value-added to your
original premise. More than likely, it will.

The following are two examples of research blunders—one my fault,
one not—both embarrassing and avoidable.

" BARBRA STREISAND...CROSSING THE LINE

During the aforementioned interview with Streisand for the promotion of her album HIGHER GROUND, I needed her to explain on camera what her inspiration was for the album. I asked. She began to explain by saying: "As I wrote in the liner notes. You know I wrote all of the liner notes…" And then she tweaks to the notion that I may not know that she wrote the liner notes. "Did you even read the liner notes?"

"No, I didn't," I answered honestly.

"I can't believe this," she ranted. "I wrote those liner notes and you are sitting here doing this interview asking me my inspiration and it is all right there…"

I got the idea that the interview was going to end right then and there. Even the crew looked like I had blown it. So, I threw a Hail Mary pass and pulled an excuse out of thin air. "Barbra, do you want to know why I didn't read your liner notes?"

She looked at me…"I didn't read them because I didn't want to fall in love with the songs because you did. I wanted to love them because I do." Even the crew sighed.

She smiled. "I understand," she said. "But I would like you to read them and call me and see if we agree." Lesson learned. 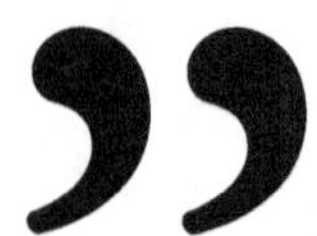

GEORGE BENSON...R.I.P.

I was excited to interview George Benson. His GEORGE BENSON COLLECTION album got me through a lot of tough nights in college. So, when the opportunity came up to do the interview live for British morning television, I thought I was ready. My producer had done a pre-interview and handed me research cards which I read and found fascinating. One specific bullet point I would be interested in talking about was that he had ten sons and they had all gone into the music business. I thought that would be a great piece of conversation.

George is a mellow sort of interview. No highs, no lows...just even keel. We got the signal that we were live, and I dove right in, thanking him for my college experience with his album and then following up with his ten sons in the music business. "You must be so proud?"

"Well one of them is dead," he simply said.

Now that would have been a piece of information I may have needed to know...don't you think? I was dumbfounded and wasn't sure where to go with that. I fumbled, "Of course, I meant no disrespect. But so many of your sons in the business must be heartwarming." The interview went on but I was thrown. The moral of that story is to do your own research or at the very least, double-check the facts. It wasn't the producer who looked incompetent on live television...it was me.

FIND SOMETHING RELATABLE/PERSONABLE

In doing your research, you may find some information about your interviewee that you find interesting, unusual, or common ground with. You can use that to establish a pre-interview report or relationship. Or perhaps that information could enhance the motivation of why your interviewee did or did not do one thing or another.

The following is a good example of how that worked for me.

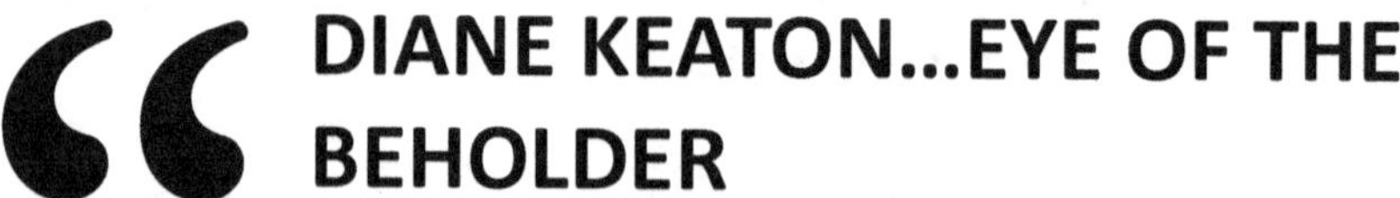

DIANE KEATON...EYE OF THE BEHOLDER

I was interviewing Diane Keaton, known for being flighty and scattered, for the movie MARVIN'S ROOM and when watching the film, I noticed Keaton had just a micro pause before each line. I fixated on it. So, when it came time for the interview, I had a thought. As we were prepping the lights and the microphones, I said to her that I noticed the pause. She was taken aback. I knew I was on to something.

We started the interview and I started in right away with the pause I noticed. She said she didn't do it intentionally. I said she did. I went on to explain that I knew she was an acclaimed photographer and suggested that she was seeing the world in a series of snapshots, in portraiture, and that pause was to snap the shot. She smiled and glowed, said that no one made that observation, and was very happy I did. The interview was exceptional and more in-depth than I had ever seen her be.

THE MOST IMPORTANT PERSON IN THE ROOM IS YOU

This may seem presumptuous, but to the person you work for, it's not. You have a job to do. Get an interview, and get relevant, entertaining, or informative answers. There is no excuse to have been outwitted, intimidated, sidestepped, refused, shut down, or bullied. All of which can happen under extreme circumstances unless you recognize and remember two things:

1. They agreed to sit for an interview so they can't be completely unresponsive.

2. They are simply people with a job just like you...and yours is the more important position to your boss.

Generally, you only have to concern yourself with the power structure in the room when things get confrontational or there is an outward reluctance to answer any questions. These are my suggestions when you feel that there is reluctance or confrontation in the air:

- Remain professional and in charge. You don't want to look like you are losing your cool or are getting flustered.

- Keep the interview short and to the point.

- Do not ramble with your questions. Be concise.

- Avoid unnecessary conversation. Be cordial and polite but do not protract the situation. Get the job done and get out.

- Rephrase a question if you don't get a satisfactory answer the first time.

For example:

- Do you think the grass is greener on the other side of the fence?

- What would be appealing to you to be on the other side of the fence?

The following is possibly the most extreme example of a time when I had to remember that I had a job to do under extreme conditions. This was the worst experience in my professional interviewing career. I cite this example because I didn't crack under the pressure but it took all my professional strength not to walk away from the situation.

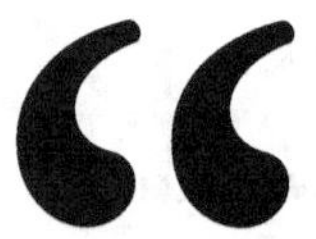

ROSEANNE...NO JOKE!

We were early days on the air with EXTRA. We needed big stars to come on the show and do interviews and appearances to give us credibility and show we were a contender on the level of the juggernaut ENTERTAINMENT TONIGHT. And it looked like that was about to happen. We booked the biggest star on prime-time television at the time, Rosanne. Her hit show was about to premiere season eight and we were granted an on-set interview with the star. The show, putting the cart before the horse promoted a "Roseanne exclusive" the entire week before we had even done the interview. That was a mistake.

Roseanne was notoriously hard to work with, reportedly firing staff members off her show for the slightest infraction and turning over personal assistants regularly. EXTRA decided it would take a specific personality to "win her over" in an interview setting. And that obligation fell to me. The executives felt I would be able to "charm" her. Warning flags went up on the day of the interview. Word came that she wanted to do the interview on the set, between tapings during the union-mandated lunch break. That meant almost two hundred crew members would have to stand on the set and watch my interview. They would not be happy. Then we were informed, she, Roseanne, wanted the entire cast on the set with her. Surely, they could not be happy about that demand. I was getting nervous that this was not going to go well.

We arrived between 4:00 and 5:00 and set up on the living room set. Two cameras—one on Roseanne and company and the other on me. The crew was obviously not happy to be standing there for the interview, but union rules demanded they be present for lighting, electrical, etc. The cast entered and sat around the set, also unhappy with the situation. When I greeted John Goodman, he would even look up to meet my face. This again was not a good sign.

Roseanne sat. I thanked everyone publicly for giving up their time and graciously allowing us to visit the set and began with: "Roseanne, you started this series with the character of a domestic goddess, the everywoman you said you were. You have had so much personal and professional success since then. As you start the show's new season, do you still relate to that domestic goddess character?"

She turned to her standing audience of crew members and screeched, "WHAT THE FUCK ARE YOU ASKING ME? I DON'T KNOW WHAT THE FUCK YOU ARE TALKING ABOUT…" With that, the crew began to laugh. It was at that point, the camera pointed at me and shifted off looking at me. The camera person said they were too nervous to watch me.

I braced myself and reiterated, "Do you not…or do you still see yourself in the character of Roseanne Connor?

I STILL DON'T KNOW WHAT THE FUCK YOU'RE ASKING ME? WHAT THE FUCK IS HE ASKING ME?"

I persisted, "How has the character evolved this season?"

"I DON'T GIVE A FUCK…"

And again…"FUCK!"

It was me who was fucked.

Again, the makeshift audience of a crew laughed and this went on for several more softball questions and profanity-laced answers. I knew my job was on the line. We at EXTRA have promoted an exclusive with Roseanne all week and there wasn't an answer I could use or even edit the profanity from.   I chose a different tact and turned to the cast and asked each what we could expect from their characters, getting mediocre answers, with the hope that Roseanne would calm down in the interim.

Getting back around, I finally asked Roseanne why she thought the audience still loved the show for which she gave a single-sentence forgettable answer that was at least television usable. At that point, knowing that I had at least one usable sound bite, I thanked everyone for their time and wrapped up the hellacious experience.

As we were packing to leave, her then-assistant came up to me and told me she thought I was the bravest man she'd ever seen. I thanked her and motioned to her publicist to get me off the sound-stage without having to go through the hostile mob of a crew who saw me as chum at this point. He escorted me to a side door and I was off.

By the time I got back to EXTRA's office, the spin doctoring from NBC had already begun as a call from the show's publicist to my bosses stated: "How dare the show send some fucking faggot over to try and charm Roseanne…" And it went downhill from there.

When I walked in, the management team stood there, waiting for a debrief. How could it have gone so badly? What did I do wrong to get her so upset? I was reminded that I had a job to do…and on first blush, I had failed. The tape spoke for itself and thank goodness I had coaxed at least one useable line out of her. And it became obvious I was the victim and we had been unreasonably set up.

I can't understand what goes through someone's hateful mind in attempting to destroy another person that way. But she didn't. Had EXTRA been more mature and situated, I would have probably told her that her language would not be tolerated and walked off the set. Perhaps today, her rant would have been the story. Then I needed a sound bite because, despite her power in the industry, the most important person in the room was me. "

BAD BEHAVIOR DOESN'T HAVE TO BE TOLERATED

Bad behavior is not always defined as a hostile interviewee. They would not be interviewed if they were completely resistant. They simply may be reticent to discuss the very information you need them to reveal or talk about. This can cause friction and a fractious environment and you won't necessarily get the outcome you need. Remember:

- TO DRIVE THE CAR

- THE MOST IMPORTANT PERSON IN THE ROOM IS YOU

I don't suggest taking on your interviewee in a confrontation. Your best bet is to find questions or common ground that works around a sensitive subject matter or issues that your interviewee is more comfortable talking about and then try to weave it back to the questions you need answering. Inevitably, during your career, you will find people who will not want to speak about something, and generally that something is why you may have wanted to speak with them in the first place. Pushing your agenda is not in your favor. It only serves to drive a wedge between you and your interview subject and alienate them. Remember you are there to establish a relationship, albeit briefly, of trust and partnership. You may be the most important person in the room but without a usable interview, the effort was for naught.

Having said the previous, the following are some personal examples of times when I broke the rules. I DO NOT RECOMMEND this behavior. But I thought you may like to see what was done when it seemed like there were very few options in front of me. I would argue in retrospect, there are always options but sometimes bad behavior is simply that...BAD.

" I MAY HAVE PUT MY JOB ON THE LINE...BUT ENOUGH WAS ENOUGH!

GEENA DAVIS

I worked for E! at the time and had been assigned to the junket interviews for a forgettable heist movie, QUICK CHANGE, starring Bill Murray and Geena Davis. We had been allotted a magnanimous fifteen minutes with the stars together. That amount of time can either fly by or be an eternity if things aren't going well.

Consider this a moment when things weren't going well.

I sat down and Geena asked what media outlet I represented. I let her know I was from E! and she groaned. She then turned to Bill and said, "Be careful what you say; they are just going to take it out of context." At the time, E! groped for "clever" ways to use all their content in new and different programming ways.

One such ill-fated idea was a segment called "Out of Context," whereby they took star answers to legitimate questions and put silly questions in front of them and made the answer look bizarre at best. It was interstitial programming—meaning a short segment that aired between long format, half-hour shows. The idea was it would provide a slice of comic relief. Geena Davis (and in all fairness, plenty of others) didn't care for the joke.
I realized at that point the interview was as good as over before it began. She would be hostile, curt, guarded, and not forthcoming.
Just as she warned Bill of my presumed double intention, of which I had none, the floor director indicated we were rolling tape.
Bill and she looked at me to begin the interview. I simply tossed my notepad in the air and declared, "I have nothing to say. You seem to

think I have come here with some sort of agenda you're not happy with. So speak if you want, don't speak if you want. But I have nothing to say."

Geena simply folded her arms and sat back. Bill panicked. "Are you seriously not going to ask us anything?" he stammered. I shook my head, no. He began to babble answers to non-existent questions and I continued to sit. Geena sitting in silence. When the fifteen minutes ended, I simply stood, picked up my notepad, and walked out. I fully expected a reprimand from the film company who instead begged me to stay and do another interview. "She is just jet lagged from having flown all night," they said begging me to stay.

"Then maybe she shouldn't be here," I said in my defense of the decline, knowing a bad interview can be worse than no interview. (As a footnote, I have subsequently met and interviewed Geena Davis several times and found her charming, intelligent, giving, and valued. I respect her immensely for her candor and the many causes she has embraced to improve industry working conditions.)

And then there was...

ERIC STOLZ

Early in my career in Hollywood, I wrote and/or produced electronic press kits or EPKs. EPKs were behind-the-scenes footage, star interviews/profiles, and pre-made news stories that were distributed by the movie studios to television stations across the country to publicize a movie about to come out. I, or the company I worked for at the time, would be hired by the studio marketing team over the course of the filming of the movie, be given favorable access to pivotal scenes for behind-the-scenes taping, and be allowed generous access to the stars for interviews. It was all about promoting the movie and there was no hidden agenda. So, everyone cooperated. Until this one time. The film was THE WATERDANCE, starring Eric Stolz and Helen Hunt. In short, the film is about a young man who, after enduring a hiking accident, has to face his life-altering paralysis.

What was particularly interesting was that Stolz had completely embraced the role so much so that he lived in a wheelchair for months to prepare and converted his car and home to accommodate this new living situation. This would make for interesting conversation during the interview…or so I thought. Eric Stolz, it turned out, was notoriously private and felt that if you asked a personal question, he wouldn't answer. Instead, he would hum as if to disregard your presence. I had been warned he was private but surely, I thought he would be amenable to promoting his movie and willing to explain his process in developing the character. But question after question, such as, "I gather you have adapted your life to a wheelchair to understand your character better. Could you tell me about that process?" were met with humming. Now, I was not some probing journalist; the movie company hired me to market the movie. So I took matters into my own hands. In mid-hum, I turned to the cameraman and told him to stop taping.

"Listen to me," I began, leaning in. "You can stop that fucking humming right now. If you have a problem with me or the questions that I am asking you can treat me like the professional I am and say, 'I would prefer not to answer that question.' But I am here to help you promote this movie, not to pry into your personal life. So you can cut the bullshit right now. I am not the enemy. Now act like a professional, or I will walk and won't give a shit as to what happens to your movie."

Without missing a beat and not allowing him to respond, I turned to the cameraman and instructed him to start rolling again. "Now,

I gather you have adapted your living situation to a wheelchair to embrace your character. Can you tell me about that process?"

Needless to say, I took a huge risk.

It could have gone one of two ways. He could have gotten up, had me banned from the set, and ended my job and presumably my association with the movie company. Or he could have done what he chose to do. He answered the question—rambling on eloquently and anecdotally about the process and subsequently answered all of my questions for the next forty-five minutes without a hum. It was actually enlightening and entertaining…just what the publicity team was looking for in the first place.

It's always interesting what can happen when you work together for a common goal.

At some point, when an interview is being irrational or simply unco-operative to a point where you will have nothing to left and you are rendered impotent, you have nothing to lose but to 'gently' remind them you, too, have a job to do.

All of that was followed by a "sour" note…

JULIAN LENNON

It was early for all of us. The show went on the air at 7:00 am. I was doing the British equivalent of TODAY or GOOD MORNING AMERICA called GMTV. I covered Hollywood and entertainment for them but quickly became popular as the wacky American on British morning television. As such, I found myself for the better part of the summer in a seventeen-bedroom, twenty-six-bathroom, villa in Marbella on the beachfront of the Spanish Mediterranean doing a version of the program we affectionately referred to as "FUN IN THE SUN." On any

given day, we flew in celebrities and musical guests for interviews
and performance segments. On this particular day, the guest was
Julian Lennon and I was to interview him before his performance.
Colorful language aside, I was warned that the interview would be
tough as he was being uncooperative and for lack of a better term,
unpleasant. What Julian failed to realize was that we had a past, he
and I. One of my dearest friends, Andrew Wainrib, owned one of
the most popular nightclubs in Los Angeles in its day, TRINITY. I was,
to say the least, a frequent flier, as was Julian who was purport-
edly having a "thing" with the hostess—Jade Barrymore, mother of
Drew. I said to the GMTV producer I would take care of the "Julian"
problem and he would be fine by the time we went to air.

I met Julian in the makeup room. He was, as expected, sullen and
not very personable. I introduced myself and told him that I would
be interviewing on the air. Again, he was nonplussed. I went on
to explain that we knew each other from Los Angeles. He looked
up. "Do you remember the Trinity days...like I remember the Trinity days? Perhaps we should talk about that..." He looked sheep-
ish. "I tell you what," I continued and leaned in. "You either change
your attitude and show some enthusiasm for being here or we can
talk about our past." With that, I got up and left. I let the producer
know he would be fine but there wasn't a whole lot of belief behind
that assurance.

When the time came, Julian sat on the sofa next to me. I said nothing as we waited for the cue from the director that we went live.
And with that, I began with something akin to, "We are happy to
be here this morning with Julian Lennon. Now before we begin, I
should mention that Julian and I have a past. We used to hang out
in the same club in Los Angeles." His eyes grew wide. "But we could
go on forever with old Hollywood stories, let's talk
about what you're up to today..." He couldn't have
been nicer or chattier.

DON'T BE AFRAID TO HAVE FUN…BUT…

Playfulness and familiarity is a skill that is honed. You have to read the room to know just how far you can push the limits. But I come from the school of thought that the more you can make your subject matter feel comfortable the better. Interviews can be monotonous, the more you can make them entertaining, interesting, learned, and/or comfortable, the better they will turn out.

- Early on in my career, just out of college, I made a good call with Faye Dunaway when just before walking into the room I asked an assistant if I should address her as Faye or Miss Dunaway. She said, "Miss Dunaway." When I went in, I stuck out my hand and introduced myself to Miss Dunaway. She smiled and said, "Call me Faye." She felt that I had respected her and was willing to let her hair down from there. Had I walked in as a young reporter and simply said, "Hello Faye" she may have reacted coldly and distantly. We had a lovely conversation from there on.

- Similarly, not too many months later, I was interviewing Ted Shackelford on the set of the very popular prime-time soap opera KNOTS LANDING. Things were going along very well. He was talkative and jovial. Until…during the interview, a silk light scrim blew over and the silk portion bounced on his head causing him to dramatically wince. Reacting to his clear over-reaction, I blurted out, "Now that is some acting!" He went ballistic, claiming how dangerous the situation was and how I disregarded his safety and his injury. The interview did not go well from that point on.

There is a fine line between being playful and being disrespectful. If you cross it, you are jeopardizing the interview and more importantly your job. Is it worth the risk? Only if the end product will be better

served to show your subject matter in a new or different light.
My suggestions:

1. Let the subject matter dictate just how comfortable you can
   be with the interviewee.

   a. Entertainment or lifestyle subject matter is more ame-
      nable to a free flow than business-oriented material.

2. Is your interview more comfortable on a first-name basis
   rather than a title such as Mr./Ms./Dr.? That will dictate the
   respect factor.

3. Is the setting more comfortable like a park or home rather
   than an office or place of business? The setting will connote
   formality.

4. Does your interviewee have an agenda?

   a. Are they trying to get a message out that is unbending or
      specific?

   b. You will have to work around their needs and respect why
      you have agreed to participate in the interview.

5. Pre-interview/pre-plan the interview agenda with the subject.

   a. Letting people know what you have in mind gets them
      involved rather than surprising or letting them feel am-
      bushed.

" A FRIEND IN NEED...

I got a call on Friday from a good friend of mine at Disney international marketing asking for last min-ute favor. Could I give up Saturday day off to interview the stars of BEAUTY AND BEAST: AN ENCHANTED CHRISTMAS, the straight-to-video follow-up animated feature? Ugh, I thought to myself. I never saw the first movie, won't have time to see the second, and frankly don't care to make a segment about this lackluster straight-to-video non-starter. But he was a friend, so the best I could muster was, "Who are the stars?" Tim Curry played an evil pipe organ; Robbie Benson was yet again the Beast and Paige O'Hara was the Beauty. Well, Tim Curry and I had forged a professional friendship over the years, and I thought it would be great to see him again, so I said, "Sure."

Knowing Tim has a wicked sense of humor and the fine folks at Dis-ney do not, I came up with a plan to either have fun or be bounced from the interview in one fell swoop. Harkening back to a friend of mine who once asked Miss Piggy—the oft-spurned lover of Kermit the Frog—during a Disney junket interview, if she'd ever had a frog in her throat. That single question got the interview stopped and my friend was banned for life from Disney interviews. I sat down with Tim, and after niceties, I began the interview with, "When you play the organ, does size matter?"

He answered a very playful yes to which I followed up with "Is your organ a big one?" And we went on for some time with double-meaning questions, clearly not meant for the young folks BEAUTY AND THE BEAST would attract. Then he dropped this in my lap...as it were. "If you want to talk about large organs, you should talk to Robbie Benson."

With the interview over and convinced I was done forever with Disney, I went to the door, opened it, and found my friend and the rest of the Disney international marketing team standing abreast. Oh, dear. "Marc," my friend began as I assumed my time with Disney was officially over, "that was the funniest interview we have ever watched. Can we have a copy of that tape?" Unbeknownst to me, the team had been screening my interview in another room the entire time. I was in the clear. Which only added fuel to the fire.

When I sat with Robbie Benson, the interview was also with Paige O'Hara with whom I had no interest. I surreptitiously told the cameraman to stay only on Robbie and ignore Paige and began with: "When I was talking to Tim, who plays the pipe organ, he says organ size matters. But if I want to talk about big organs I should be talking to you, Robbie.

"That is true," Robbie blushed.

With that, Paige exclaimed. "You can't say that." And I gave her a look that clearly indicated her opinion didn't matter. She huffed and Robbie just laughed.

My interview was as good as done. I had what I needed. And if you are wondering if I turned that interview into a segment...I did. The lesson learned here: you can have fun given you know the parameters, know how far you can take it, know when to pull back and be ready to pay the consequences if it goes wrong.

TELL THE STORY

Whether you are a budding reporter or a YouTube entrepreneur you need to engage the audience. And that comes down to how good of a storyteller you are. And the basis of a good story? Good writing. I suggest before you turn on the camera you put your fingers on the keyboard or pen to paper and start to write. Crafting what you want to say will save you a great deal of time and effort later on and make you a more compelling performer on camera.

WRITING FOR TELEVISION IS WRITING

The difference in writing for television is there are visuals involved. But that doesn't mean the fundamentals can be ignored. The following are my tips for television storytelling:

1. NEEDS A BEGINNING MIDDLE AND AN END

    a. All good storytelling has a story arc. Try and think about that even with internet segments.

    b. Non-linear editing can be an effective storytelling tool. For example: Asking one question, getting multiple answers, and splicing them together to make one continuous answer.

3. PEOPLE TELL YOU NOT TO USE PUNS, ALLITERATION, OR CLICHES...I LOVE THEM

    Why? People remember them, relate to them, and tweak to them.

4. VISUALS ARE PART OF THE WRITING PROCESS

    a. You can use pictures to emphasize a point you are making.

    b. Make sure you write to the picture and that the picture is an example of what you are saying.

1. COMMENTARY OR ANECDOTES MUST STAY ON POINT
    Introduce your point, make the point, and bring the point to a
    conclusion.

2. MAKING SOMETHING OUT OF NOTHING
    Sometimes you are given an assignment which is simply a sug-
    gestion or a premise, what do you do? Unless you are lying,
    you can create a supposition story.

" GERI HALLIWELL...SPICING UP HOLLYWOOD

All I was told was that Geri Halliwell—aka Ginger Spice—was on her way to Los Angeles to do a story on what she could be doing in Hollywood. Huh?!? I found out the plane she was coming in on and did what the British media (as I was working for the Brits at the time) and staked out her arrival at LAX.

While I thought I was the only one with the scoop on the plane and had been standing alone with my cameraman, by the time she came out of the VIP international tunnel, the paparazzi came out of the woodwork and descended upon her, dragging me along with them. As she was whisked to a waiting limo, my mic chord somehow got entangled with her security team and I found myself right next to her, so I asked, "What brings you to Los Angeles?" She burst into tears and my story had begun.

It was pure speculation, and I had nothing to go on except a now-surfaced rumor that she was up for the role in a CHARLIE'S ANGELS movie. Okay. That alone did not flesh out my assignment. What ensued was an odyssey of standups whereby I simply suggested several ideas of what Geri might do while she was in town, including a run in a small theater to earn her acting chops, appearing in drag to emphasize how difficult it is to play a lady cop and ending the entire segment with a strong suggestion that she simply peruse the "help wanted" ads as that was how she became a Spice Girl in the first place. The entire segment was pure commentary, based completely on crazy speculation and no facts, but was pure entertainment. The point is...clever writing and storytelling can "spice" up a non-starter—making something out of nothing.

KNOW WHEN ENOUGH IS ENOUGH

SELF-EDITING IS THE HARDEST THING TO DO

We all believe that everything we say is valuable, informative, entertaining, defining, or instructive. But the truth is sometimes we are simply long-winded, tangential, obtuse, unclear, and rambling. Fitting everything you want or need to say into a designated time frame is a skill set that requires discipline and practice.

As mentioned, each segment—whether an hour or a minute—tells a story, with a beginning, middle, and end. But it is much harder to tell that story in a news average of ninety seconds than it is in thirty minutes. Why? Because thirty minutes allows for sound bites to breathe, pacing to be woven in, and explanations and descriptors to be inserted. In ninety seconds, you have to do the same thing but be straight to the point—truncated sound bites, clever use of visuals with specific descriptive narration, and impactful on-camera standups.

It is always better to have too much to choose from, than too little to work with. How you choose to craft that storytelling is the art. The following are my suggestions to help you determine when enough is enough:

1. ARE YOU BEING REPETITIVE?
   Have you made your point earlier? Or have you expressed the same thing with a different example?

2. IS WHAT YOU ARE SAYING VALUE ADDED?
   If it doesn't move the narrative along, does it need to be there?

3. ARE YOU BEING GRATUITOUS JUST TO BE A CAMERA HOG?
   When it comes to talent being on camera, is it necessary? My philosophy is that the talent should only be on camera to give information that couldn't be given with other experts or visuals.

4. THE AUDIENCE DOESN'T KNOW WHAT YOU EDITED OUT.
   You have to make tough decisions when you edit—this pretty picture or that one, this sound bite or that one. You love them all. But they don't all fit in the segment. You have to make a choice. But the audience will never know what the other option was. Feel confident that you made the right choice.

5. CAN YOU COMBINE INFORMATION TO MAKE A STRONGER POINT? Are there facts that, when combined, strengthen the segment and take up less time to explain?

Overall. Have you said what you needed to say...beginning, middle, and end?

RADIO

RADIO

PART ONE:

THESE DAYS

Someone I respect within the entertainment industry recently told me that radio is dying. Really?!? Consolidations have made it a tougher industry but…dying? Here are just a few facts as accumulated by Statista:

"Radio is one of the most powerful mediums in the United States, with a weekly reach of around 82.5 percent among adults. There are over 15,445 radio stations in the U.S., all competing for a piece of this massive market. WTOP, a station operating out of Washington D.C. is the largest of its kind in the U.S., pulling in 62 million U.S. dollars in yearly revenue. Online radio is also playing an increasing role in the radio market, with an estimated 974 minutes spent listening to online radio every month in 2021.

American radio stations generated total revenue of over 10 billion U.S. dollars in 2020, of which 940 million dollars was generated through online radio streaming. In addition to the massive national stations and broadcasts, local public radio stations also appear to be thriving. Public radio station revenue has decreased from around 12.8 billion U.S. dollars in 2019 to an estimated 11.7 billion in 2021. 'Country' is by far the most popular format, with 2,200 individual stations broadcasting music from this genre. As of 2020, Americans averaged 99 minutes of radio listening time per day, with much of this time being spent while commuting."

- IHeartRadio is the biggest online radio company in the United States by a significant margin owning 863 stations.

- Most popular genre for ages 18-24: Rhythmic.

- Average daily time listening to the radio in the U.S.: 99 minutes.

- Average weekly time listening to online radio: 974 minutes.

WHY IS RADIO STILL WORKING?

92% of Americans still listen to radio every week, which is close to 300 million people. Radio reaches 90% of adults 18-34, 94% aged 35-49, and 91% aged 50 and older. Why is that? These simple facts should shed some light:

- There is portability to radio—it is in cars, on apps, cell phones, and other devices.

- Traditional radio is free, unlike cable television.

- Radio is adaptable—now available through laptops, computers, cell phones, and smart speakers so you never have to be far from your favorite station.

- Radio is inclusive, drawing listeners across all demographics:

  ◊ Attracting 99% of Hispanic Americans

  ◊ 98% of African Americans

  ◊ 98% of women aged 25-54

  ◊ 93% of teens aged 12-17

THE DIFFERENCE IN RADIO

TERRESTRIAL
With terrestrial radio broadcasting, the radio waves are broadcast by a land-based radio station. Stations are often affiliated with a network of several stations which provide content in a common format, either in broadcast syndication or both. Radio stations broadcast in one of two ways: AM or FM. AM radio stations transmit in amplitude modulation while FM radio stations transmit in frequency modulation, which is older analog audio standards.

AM stations were the earliest broadcasting stations to be developed. AM broadcasts occur in the medium wave frequency range of 525 to 1,705 kHz also known as the "standard broadcast band". FM occurs on VHF airwaves in the frequency range of 88 to 108 MHz By the 1980s, since almost all new radios included both AM and FM tuners, FM became the dominant medium, especially in cities. Because of its greater range, AM remained more common in rural environments.

WHAT ARE YOUR OPTIONS TO WORK IN RADIO?
Besides upper management, there is the news or music director, journalists, hosts, producers, marketers, system engineers, writers, social media coordinators, and sales personnel, to name the obvious. Why name all these jobs you may not be interested in when all you want to do is to get paid to talk? Well, talking is just part of the process of studio production. And many hosts have gotten in front of the mic by starting behind the scenes. Options may include:

Acquiring content

- Downloading songs from the internet.

- Ripping CDs.

- Recording audio in and out of the studio for instance when the reporters conduct interviews.

- Third-parties sources such as syndicated shows.

- Submissions from artists or record promoters.

Production

- Developing show concepts.

- Creating radio imaging.

- Coming up with scripts.

- Booking on-air guests.

- Preparing and editing reports, interviews, news segments, and other show items.

- Adding information to a track such as artist details, setting cue points & creating categories.

Scheduling/Programming

- Creating daily schedules.

- Scheduling promotions, advertising, and on-air announce-ments, typically done by the traffic department.

- Deciding when to air programs.

- Creating playlists.

- Setting up rotations (templates).

- Setting up interviews.

- Preparing program logs.

- Voice tracking.

- Screening phone calls.

On-air tasks

- Introducing and interviewing guests.

- Executing shows.

- Posting show updates on social media, Facebook and Twitter.

- Cueing and introducing upcoming music tracks.

- Promoting the station's programming through hooks, cross-promotion, etc.

- Enforcing the station's identity by announcing the station's call letters.

- Conducting surveillance of the weather, traffic, time, and temperature checks.

WHAT IS AN ACTUAL RADIO STATION?

There are several different kinds of radio stations: Pirate, Community, Internet, Hospital, Digital, and Commercial). What a D.J. or host is looking to work in is considered commercial...generally advertiser based with call letters beginning with "K" or "W". But when we talk about working in a radio station, we are talking about working in a radio studio. And in that case, we must differentiate between a self-operated studio versus a tech-operated studio.

- SELF-OPERATED STUDIO:
  The D.J. or host/presenter operates the equipment. Commercial studios commonly have this setup and producers, with the guests and/or co-hosts in the same room.

- TECH-OPERATED STUDIO:
  In this setup, a technician or producer controls the programming from a second control room.

  Studios also fall into these categories:

  - ON-AIR STUDIOS
    This is used for live broadcasts. Many times this is set up
    as a self-operated situation.

  - PRODUCTION STUDIOS
    This studio deals with content that is not live: commer-
    cials, promos, news packages, etc. In many cases, this
    studio can act as a backup for the On-Air studio if similarly
    equipped.

  - SOUND STUDIOS
    This is to record voice-over tracks or instrumental sounds
    for pre-recorded segments or production.

  - CONTROL ROOM
    A control room allows for the mixer to be in a separate
    room and allows for a producer to do that task, leaving
    the host free to...well...talk. This is an ideal situation for
    talk radio formats or multiple guest situations.

WORKING FOR A STATION GROUP

Several radio stations can be owned by one owner. That is considered
a station group and station group ownership is now considered the
norm. The benefit of working for a station group is that your program
can be distributed over several stations and several markets, growing
your fan base. While your deal may preclude you from profiting from
multi-station airings, you do win in the end by being able to exploit
the listener base on social media or personal appearances.

SYNDICATION

WHAT IS SYNDICATED PROGRAMMING?

Broadcast syndication is the practice of leasing the right to broadcasting radio programs to multiple television stations and radio stations, without going through a broadcast network.

WHAT IS THE POINT OF BRINGING IN SYNDICATED PROGRAMMING?

Local programming has certain expenses associated with it: talent, studio overhead, etc. If you can buy in a ready-made program at a reasonable rate, it can be cheaper than paying to produce your own. High-profile programs, with notable talent charge rates for market size and command higher advertising rates for a devoted fan base. The following are a couple of examples of nationally syndicated personalities that rate high locally:

1. RYAN SEACREST:
    Pop music format—Day part: Various

2. JOHN TESH:
    Advice talk/music format—Day part: Afternoon

3. DELILAH:
    Relationship advice/talk/music format—Day part: Nights

SIDEBAR: BARRY SCOTT— "THE LOST 45's"

Barry Scott has a resume that can be essentially narrowed down to one line, one title, one show: "The Lost 45's"—now forty years on traditional radio station broadcast and then national syndication. Not bad for the kid who knew from the age of five who, with a cassette recorder, created his first radio air-check complete with DJ prowess as he introduced Herb Alpert hits and rounded it out with a weather segment. Never having wavered in his radio dreams, by high school, he was interning at the local radio station. But it was during his studies at the prestigious Emerson College in Boston, that an idea came to mind. Whatever happened to those 'one hit wonders', those popular songs of the 70s and 80's which simply hit big and fell off the playlist? And that was the inspiration and launch of "The Lost 45's" on Emerson College radio, WERS, where the show received national press awareness. Upon graduation and reporting for work at the then WZLX, the nation's first classic hits format station, he did what any enterprising artist would do—he pitched his program. It's been on a Boston radio station ever since. From having placed the show on eight different radio stations in Boston, to national syndication on 80-100 stations, "The Lost 45's" has not been lost for four decades.

Why syndication and how did it happen for you?
"Syndicated DJs have a rabid audience following because they have a niche. You are offering something different on that radio station. I had written a book about "The Lost 45's", so there was some national attention. I had been looking for a syndicator for some time. And there is no trick to it. Your presentation has to express the passion and reality of why this format works. Station managers, who inevitably will place your program, have to believe putting something different on their air will attract the audience. You have to sell the why as much as the what?"
"In my case, I got incredibly lucky. My show aired on Sunday nights in Boston. Driving through the city on the way back to New York one Sunday evening was a radio syndicator, who just so happened to listen to the show. He contacted the station to see if the show was available and life in syndication began in 1996."

"But, I will tell you that even with a syndicator, I faced obstacles.

The first was my voice. I don't have that traditional booming voice that went with radio in the 1980s. I have a softer more resonant tone. Radio stations were unsure that an audience would relate to that. I like to refer to the quirky tone of the late Kasey Kasem who was hugely successful in syndication with "America's Top 40" and how his voice became a signature. Now, to this day, I am recognized in public, for my voice. But it was a hard sell back then. The other obstacle is that my program was an unproven format, in terms of a national rollout. You can be the big fish in your local pond. But many station managers said there was a reason these songs were one and done—people didn't like them. The truth was they were chart-topping songs of the day that simply fell through the cracks. And what I found with my program; people loved the nostalgia behind them. My show offered insight and fun facts behind the song and each week had a named guest for an interview."

After years of working with a syndicator, you broke off and now self-syndicate. How and why?
"With traditional syndication, you get paid from a percentage of the advertising profits. With the consolidation of radio to large-scale station owners, those percentages have been skewed out of favor of the talent. I took the show back, which could be a risk, but I under-stood I had a long-term relationship with the stations on which I aired, and the show was a proven success.

So, what I did was offer the station a full 100% of the advertising dollars in exchange for a stipend or to pay to air the show. This is risky in today's market where budgets have been squeezed. Even with the drop in market count, this scenario has proven a more prof-itable solution. Similarly, my show airs on the weekends. I re-air the show on Mondays on my website for a subscription charge. These days there are creative ways on different platforms to find second-ary income channels."

What do you see for the future?
"Program directors are already testing the notion that the 70s are just too long ago. Today's "kids" don't relate. Well, the truth, again, is the number one demographic for radio listeners is ages 50 and above. The "kids" today are streaming and doing other things to get their music fix. Will I have to morph the show? That is still to be determined. But until then, I'll keep "Da Doo Run Run"ing along. I do hope everyone gets the reference that, that was a hit by Shawn Cassidy in 1977."

And for those with a creative entrepreneurial spirit for syndication, Scott has these tips:

- *LISTENERS CAN POINT THE WAY*
  Many times, your format is quite on point. Audience feedback, if taken seriously, will get you to hone and polish your show so it is ready for a national audience.

- *DON'T TAKE "NO" FOR AN ANSWER...YET*
  The right guest. The right topic. These can sway a decision even if they are presented in a format that has already been pitched. Be persistent and know when there is an opportunity to re-introduce...and I mean re-introduce, not re-pitch...the product. Show that each episode is fresh and provides value to lure return listeners.

- *ADAPT TO THE MARKETPLACE AND THE TIME*
  Your show may be right in one market and not in another. Is there a way to easily tweak content for the market or the time slot? You are not an a la carte broadcaster, but you may find you can be flexible.

- *BELIEVE IN THE PRODUCT*
  You can't sell what you don't believe is fundamentally good

or right. For every reason why not to move forward, give them the counter-reasoning. Many station managers didn't believe that people cared about what they considered "has been" music. I reminded and reiterated about popularity then, the nostalgia now, and that 80% of what they were quick to discard as "Lost…for a reason…45's" were top 40 chart hits. Some people need convincing, but they won't be convinced if you don't believe.

- *KEEP IT FRESH*
Although it is format-based programming, there are plenty of things you can do to keep topics fresh and programs stimulating and entertaining. In my case two examples come to mind:

  ◊ *When Irene Cara passed away, I quickly put together a tribute show. Local programmers can do that kind of turnaround with their existing formats. I can.*

  ◊ *In forty years, I had never done an Elvis show. Because he was dead by 1977, long before I could have interviewed him. But I realized he put out many hits in the 70s and many of the talent I had interviewed over the years named or referred to Elvis as some sort of inspiration. I put together a show, not about Elvis per se, but about how Elvis influenced so many others.*
  It was a hit.

  In both cases, I took the opportunity to offer a fresh new program within my existing format.

SATELLITE

Satellite radio, while popular with advertising-free channels and high-profile personalities having been lured to the format such as Howard Stern, growth has been stunted by two factors:

1. The enormous cost of launching space-based transmitters.

2. Restrictions on radio spectrum licenses in the United States.

   As a result, there are two options for your listening options:

   - SIRIUS

   - XM

WHAT IS THE VALUE OF SATELLITE RADIO?

There are several differences between satellite radio and traditional terrestrial radio. Many believe the differences are for the better:

1. EXPANSE:
   Since satellite radio uses satellites, it can broadcast its programming throughout the entire country and not just locally. This is appealing for the high-profile presenters to acquire and maintain maximum audiences.

2. FEE VS. FREE:
   This is also why satellite radio is a subscription fee-based service which unlike local free radio keeps advertising to a minimum.

3. VARIETY:
   Satellite offers a larger number of stations to choose from.

4. QUALITY:
   The sound quality is consistent and better than radio which can fluctuate depending on far from the radio station you are.

PART TWO:

GETTING IN IT...TO WIN IT!

Those starting out fall into two categories: College trained and Self-taught.

CLASSICALLY TRAINED/EDUCATED:

By this, it is meant to indicate those who went to college, university, or trade school to learn the craft of radio. At such schools, students learn the technical aspects of how radio works: working with the board, etc. And as such, have practiced their skills as hosts, presenters, etc., and may present well-polished air-checks for submissions for jobs. But in this ever-changing world of radio, many schools are no longer offering a major in radio communications. As such, are students truly being taught the nuance of being an on-air talent? That's where we come in.

LOOKING TO BE A PERSONALITY?

ARE YOU THE NEXT RYAN SEACREST, WENDY WILLIAMS, RUSH LIMBAUGH, OR HOWARD STERN?

The first thing it is worth pointing out is you can't teach people to be natural. What their education gave them are credentials that get them in the door. They still have to have "it", that certain something that makes an audience respond. And it is even harder in radio to a degree than television because you aren't seen. You are doing it all with your voice. You have to paint a picture and tell a story, create a character that people want to like and come back to for more. You won't find it in a textbook. You won't find it in a classroom.

QUALITIES TO LOOK FOR:

- WHAT DEFINES A GOOD VOICE?
  People used to say: "You have a great voice for radio." And what that usually meant is that you had one of those announcer voices—booming or deep and bass. That is great for voice-over talent. But these days all kinds of voices are needed on the radio—from male and female to ethnic and urban. The bottom line is not who you are but what you are. Does your voice match the content you are presenting; the format you represent? Are you understood when you speak? If you are an irritant to someone you will always be an irritant. Do you come across as personable and relatable? Your voice is your calling card, your character. Because you are not seen, it defines you. To that end, define it.

- WHO ARE YOU?
  You can manipulate your character by manipulating your voice. If you are trying to be sultrier or sexy, you can incorporate a whispery, more resonant tone. If you want to be more authoritarian, be sharp and direct. But there is a difference between mystique and mistake. Do not create a character where a character is not needed. When in doubt, defer to your natural self.

  Remember the audience is going to invest in what you put out there. You can create a sultry diva named "Miss Understood" and she is the queen of late-night love advice call-in between love song favorite tunes. But you have to live up to that character in public appearances and potentially market that character on social media. Can you do it? It can be fun...but it will work.

- WHAT IS AN ASSET?

  An accent, a rasp, a resonance, a baritone...all of these can be an asset if you use them to your advantage. Make them part of the personality you are creating. Individuality is what makes you stand out and you only have your voice to rely on. But it means nothing if you don't use it correctly. When you have an original-sounding voice, you may have to concentrate on clarity more than perhaps someone else. To that end, think of the rules of voice-over work, and that should help you define and polish your asset:

  a. BE FLEXIBLE

  Use your range as best as possible.

  b. ENUNCIATE

  Make sure you are pronouncing your words correctly and clearly. This is key to not losing credibility If you are trying to convey a message or company brand. Should you be reading from a script and a word is unfamiliar, write it out phonetically so you don't stumble over the pronunciation.

  c. APPROPRIATE PACING

  Think of your work as a performance that requires a rhythm and tempo. Your pacing can be part of the creative process.

  d. VOICE ACTING

  Does your voice require a certain amount of acting? And by that, have you created a character that is a little over the top or stretches the boundaries that may allow you to get away with a little more playfulness? If so, go for it. But remember to be mindful of your presentation. You still need to reach your audience.

  e. BE NATURAL

  Nothing beats the real you. Be as natural a performer as

you can be. Even if you are acting a little, be as natural as
you can with your delivery.

WHAT DEFINES A GOOD PERSONALITY?

A good radio personality is quite simply a person with a solid personality. Are you someone who is outgoing or commands the room?
That kind of high energy can translate to the studio. You are not
afraid to command the conversation. You are charismatic. The secret
is to channel that through the mechanics of the medium. Have something to say and the conviction to say it.

- Life experience... matters. You must have more to say than
  just fun facts. Be willing to share anecdotes and stories about
  yourself so that the audience can relate to who you are as a
  person and not just an announcer.

WHEN PEOPLE COME TO NIKI:

As a consultant for nearly 10 years, Niki has come across all kinds of
talent--both polished and novice. But consistently, talent benefits
from the same lessons—even those with college degrees. I generally ask introspective questions—getting talent to polish their skills
by looking inside. Then we focus on basics everyone practices most
people don't realize they are faulting on. The following are a few of
my tried and tested bullet points that make even seasoned performers think again:

- WHAT DO YOU WANT PEOPLE TO THINK, FEEL, AND SPEAK
  ABOUT YOU AFTER THEY HAVE HEARD YOU ON AIR?

  I ask this question because it reminds the talent that they are
  leaving an impression on the audience. What do they want
  that impression to be? This thought process will allow the
  talent—even the most outrageous shock jock—to think and

hone their presentation to make sure they come across as they think they come across. Listen to your airchecks. Did you sound like you thought you did? If not, how did it differ? Make notes and listen to your feedback.

- WHEN YOU HEAR A SONG, WHAT DO YOU SAY ABOUT IT?
This exercise is not as much about the content but about the presentation. Are you entertaining? Are you enthusiastic about what you are saying? Do you care? If you don't, the audience won't either. You are driving the bus. Keep the personality strong. And when it comes to content there are some common mistakes:

- SAYING TOO MUCH
Give one point for each break. If you are talking about an artist's look on a red carpet, do not also mention the new car they just bought and then the restaurant they were just seen coming out from. It is too much information. Stick with one point and make it entertaining.

- NOT USING CONTENT AS A TRANSITION
If you are giving a fun fact about the artist you just heard from, ideally it should transition into a fun fact about the artist you are just about to hear. In other words: So if you talking about the dress one singer was seen in on the red carpet transition to "but the fashionista gracing the cover of this month's XXX magazine is our next artist...."

  ◊ BEING BORING
  Don't drone on. Keep the beat. Think of your delivery as music.

- HOW CAN YOU SPEAK WITH FEWER WORDS?
Word economy is important. You will want to avoid filler words (we will touch on this later) and avoid repeating words or points. You will want to get to the point. Why is this impor-

tant? Radio moves fast, and the audience tends to be multi-tasking. The audience can have a limited attention span. They do not want to be bored. Hit quickly and directly. But avoid the most common mistake: talking too fast.

After I work on these questions, I work on pacing, cadence, and inflection. (Again, we will touch on these issues a little later in this section.)

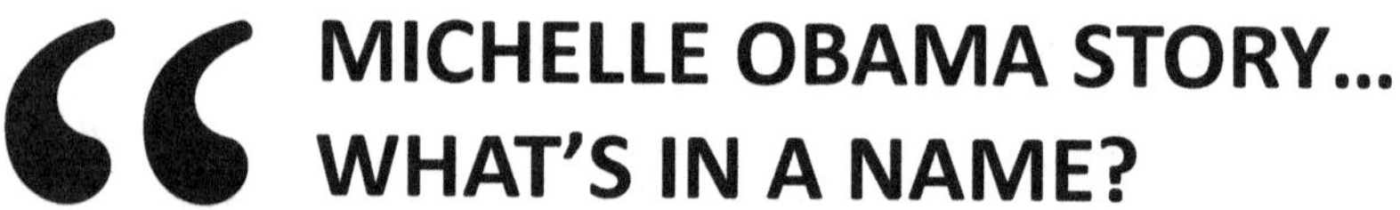

MICHELLE OBAMA STORY... WHAT'S IN A NAME?

Well The first thing I'll say, is that I'm really glad some names don't stick!

If the first radio name that I had given myself stuck, instead of knowing me as "First Lady Niki", I would be known as "Nurse Niki." Wait? What? I thought I was being so clever. What happened was, I chose "Nurse Niki" as a sign-off at the end of an email I sent for an audition. The idea was that I was going to be the medicine or antidote to making a successful show. "Nurse Niki" was here to make things better. Well, I was no prescription for success...but I did get the gig. Fortunately, the host of the show, "Flying Brian", saw through my band-aid brandishing "Nurse Niki" and gave me the official and, might I add the fabulous, name "First Lady Niki!"

How regal did that sound? I began to envision myself riding in cars waving at people like a parade attraction. I started to think I had to live up to a reputation I didn't have yet. But it was empowering, and I was determined to rise to the role. What I didn't know is that a stamp of approval would elevate exponentially! Fast forward to

2009, just days before the presidential election, and a last-minute interview request was made of me to interview none other than Michelle Obama. The topic was obvious: get out to vote. And she was working it...and rightfully...as her husband could potentially at that point become the first black president of the United States of America. You could say she was a motivated interviewee.

I don't get easily intimidated. But I have to admit I was a bit nervous to speak to her because in my mind I was thinking, if all goes well, this lady would potentially be the first lady of the United States. As we have all come to understand, Michelle Obama is a great conversationalist, and the interview went well. And towards the end, I couldn't help but say to her: "You could potentially be the First Lady, and shucks they called me First Lady buuuut ..."

And before I could say another word, she cuts me off and says: "Oooh the REAL First Lady". I knew the audience could feel the smile in her voice! I shove the chair back from the desk in excitement smiling and thinking if this woman becomes First Lady of the United States which, as history played out, was about to happen in less than 24 hours. She put the ultimate stamp on MY name, "First Lady Niki", playfully deferring that I came first! She was gracious to say that to me at a time in her life when she could have been anything but gracious. And because of that acknowledgment, I have tried to live up to that role professionally ever since.

What's in a name? Everything! Choose wisely. You never know who is paying attention and how it might matter. 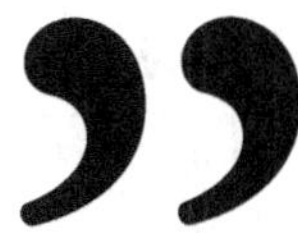

SELF TAUGHT:

HOW IT BEGAN FOR NIKI

I had always been told that I was perfect for media of some sort—hung out at the water cooler, always had the stories, was the life of the party, and was the gal everyone wanted to hang out with and was always up for a good time. When an ad popped up for a person to read the news on the radio—Wanted: a female voice. Why not me? I had no experience except to be a female, had a voice, and no fear.

The audition was obvious: consisting of reading pre-arranged news stories—but I, of course, interjected personality. Such as, there was a story about a recall on tires, and I added some pop culture references to the story without a prompt. It fits the format. And it worked.

When I knew I was going to audition, I went out every night I could and introduced myself to everyone and told everyone I was audition-ing. I was already putting myself out there. The point of that was to campaign. Getting people familiar with me and cultivating an audi-ence from the get-go. And then I went to places where the host of the show hung out and stayed there and introduced myself. I wanted to be gregarious and show I could work a crowd. Because even in radio, you are essentially working a crowd. Even with no experience, establishing yourself is essential. Now, with social media, it is more important and easier.

Some would say I got lucky. I say, I took advantage of the opportunity and saw where my abilities could fit a situation. No, I didn't get a college-trained education, but I did have what they needed: the voice, the personality, and a talent. The mechanics can be taught on the job.

Is it rare? Not necessarily. Because the industry is fluid. And with today's technology, you can create audition air checks on your computer and submit them. Be fearless.

" THERE IS A WAY TO PESTER YOUR PATH TO THE MIC

I am often asked how you get into radio. And just like the age-old question: "Hey, how can I get my song played on the radio?", it requires a long, short answer. Aside from my story of winning a radio contest and the rest being history, I would like to tell you about another fluke I've come across in my career. Not that I am advising anyone to bank on being a fluke, but I can't help but point out that finding natural talent isn't always like finding the proverbial needle in a haystack. It can be as close as the other end of a phone line.

I was doing a morning show for iHeart radio which, in between music, consisted of a discussion with a panel of lively hosts. I played the role of the moderator of the panel—the voice of reason between bigger and more blustering personalities. We had a great time and partially it was because we would have regular callers that were just GOLD! They added so much to the show with their personalities and humor or interesting points of view. We had one in particular who used to call into our show regularly. He was quick-witted, quick on his feet, and flamboyant. I say flamboyant because yes, the right over-the-top personality will translate over the radio. But moreover, he also gave us a perspective that we didn't have on the show—an openly gay representative of the LGBTQ+ community.

Some time went by and he continued to call in and we used him regularly. But not too much time later, the opportunity presented itself for the addition of a member to the show. He, it was decided, was a perfect fit—even without a radio background. What he didn't have on his resume, he more than made up for in practical smarts.

He listened to the show daily; he was familiar with our personalities; he was even familiar with the other frequent callers and he knew the flow of the show. All these things worked in his favor and he made for a perfect addition. And with his input, the show went from success to greater success.

Let's face it, that doesn't happen every day. But everyone is looking for natural talent. Because that's the one thing they can't teach you in the classroom—raw, natural talent. We don't know where the next "big thing" is coming from…but we are always looking. Is that you on the other end of the line? So if you want to be noticed… know where you want to be, do your research, and make your best efforts to be heard. Because people—the right people—are listening.

AS SUCH WHAT DOES NIKI ADVISE PEOPLE DOING IT ON THEIR OWN

These days, with social media and the ability to create audition air checks on your laptop, Niki doesn't discourage anyone from creating their radio segments and submitting them where they can for what they can. But two fundamental pieces of advice are on offer before you make any submission:

- PRACTICE, PRACTICE, PRACTICE:
  No one is or was perfect right out of the gate. Do it and then again…and again, again, and again. Be familiar with your timing, pacing, tone, intonation, content, etc. The bottom line is simply to get comfortable with talking. It is a skill.

- LISTEN TO YOURSELF:
  Do you like the sound of your voice? Were you interested in what you said? Did it make sense? Were you entertained? Could you have done it better? If you thought your performance could use improvement, then it could. Do it again…and again, until you find it comfortable to your ear. If you don't like

what you hear, why should anyone else?

HERE ARE NIKI'S TIPS:

- DEFINE WHO YOU ARE
  Deciding what you want to project is important. As mentioned, the audience can't see you. So it is important to add color to who you are. That only can come from defining your strengths.

  - ◊   Are you an expert?

  - ◊   Are you an introvert or an extrovert?

  - ◊   Do you have a skill set such as humor or advice?

  - ◊   Are you more of a co-host?

- CONTENT IS KEY
  Content is everywhere. It goes beyond the latest pop culture story you find online. You can find it in interactions with people, riding in your car listening to music, when you see or hear something that makes you laugh or cry. Content is thoughts, feelings, and angles and it is up to you to move it forward in a personal and progressive way.

  Here is an exercise to help you: Take a song from the format you are working in and think of three different fun facts or angles you can say about the artist or the work that will engage the audience. You can relate the work to today's events or even provide tangential information about the works meaning as it relates to other fun facts. Be creative. You want to be original in your content to not lose or bore an audience.

  Stay on top of trends and information.

WHY SHOULD WE LISTEN TO WHAT YOU HAVE TO SAY?
It is not about you! The big question is what is in it for the
audience. It is they who are investing their time in you. What
is the return on that investment? Are you going to entertain,
inform, inspire, connect, or persuade? Have you earned their
trust to do any of those things?

Earning trust takes time. Be consistent. They are going to
want to know about you. Don't be afraid to share interesting
anecdotes and stories about you which are appropriate and
not gratuitous. It's not about you...it's about you connection
with them.

STUDY, DON'T MIMIC
It is good to listen to others to get an idea of flow and format
and style. You can learn a lot by seeing or hearing what works
for others. But you must develop your own format and personality. It should come naturally in its basics, but the polish
should be unique to you. You don't want to be the next so
and so; you want to be the first you.

RELATIONSHIP BUILDING/CONNECTION
"A stranger is just a friend you haven't met yet." Talk to the
audience like they are already a friend. Don't forget, people
always remember how you make them feel. And if you get the
opportunity to meet them in person, treat them like a STAR!

" JENNIFER LOPEZ...
THAT LIGHTBULB MOMENT

Don't be fooled by the rock that I got I'm just a "Jenny from the Block!"

Those words just make me feel like she's one of us. One of the things I love the most about Jennifer Lopez is the fact that she has had this ability to remain relevant throughout the years by just being JLo and doesn't have to have done anything—music or movies—she just stays in the social consciousness.

What was cool for me as I prepared for our interview is that I had followed JLo go from humble beginnings, starting as a dancer on the hit 90's show IN LIVING COLOR to then killing the role in the film SELENA and going on to developing, producing, recording in television, film, and music. They call that a mogul. As a driven business-woman, her private life seemed fair game. But was it? But what I admired is it didn't seem to bother her that we were literally bothering her.

So here we are; the year is 2012, and I am told a few hours before it was even about to happen that I would have an interview with Jennifer Lopez. She was a judge on AMERICAN IDOL at the time but, more importantly, was about to embark on her first world tour. When we started our conversation, I shared some of the same reasons that I had listed above as to why I admired her. As we continued with the interview and talked about the show, I segued into questions about the upcoming tour. Ms. Lopez paused, somewhat startled, and said in a moment of genuine introspective realization: «this is my first world tour!» As an interviewer, you dream of these moments, where you can tap into a genuine reaction and have a breakthrough with a start. But even I was startled that this was the one.

Before I knew it I said: «This is your first world tour?!! You›re Jenifer Lopez. I can›t believe it! You›re a worldwide sensation!»

Again, she paused. And reality set it and she spoke with a humble tone—Jenny from the block, «Yes ...this is really my first world tour.» It felt like her silence was a big wow or a light bulb moment! And from that moment on I could feel the shift in conversation. It went from an interview to a conversation with me, just a girlfriend, who was genuinely interested in what she had to say!

I tell this story because the art of the interview is not just asking questions...it's the art of listening. If I hadn't heard her surprise and recognized her "little girl in a big world" moment...we would have lost the moment. Especially on radio, where the audience can't read body language, it is important to recognize the inflection of realization. Let's just say she never did have that reaction; I could have easily asked her: Did you ever think that Jenny from the block could extend that block around the world? That may have humbled her in the same way. You never know. But it is your job to try. Even if you think you have heard it all before, the job is about creating moments. You should always be looking for the human element and not the star-struck appeal.

PART THREE:

THE NUTS AND BOLTS OF HOW RADIO WORKS

THE MECHANICS
WORKING THE EQUIPMENT

Again, we are not here to teach you how to push the buttons and modulate the sound. There are plenty of tutorials and courses on-line and at qualified schools that can give you the DOs and DON'Ts of those "how to...s." But, what we would like to point out is that in this new world order of remote work, independent work, syndicated and internet opportunities, without a large investment, you can create a studio at home and broadcast.

To get started, you will need a computer, the internet, and a broadcast platform (Research the various platforms and what is entailed to drop your format onto them. For example, Live365.) The following is the basic equipment you need to complete your studio setup:

◊   MICROPHONE This is essential for live and recorded talk. Do not rely on built-in mics or earbuds as they will have the lowest possible quality. Dynamic mics provide a warmer more focused sound while condenser mics provide a brighter, cleaner sound. With either, check the adaptability of your equipment and power source. And you may want to consider purchasing these extra add-ons:

◊   Microphone stand

◊   Shock Mount

◊   This eliminates unwanted sounds such as mic tapping and other vibrations.

◊   Pop Filters/Windscreens
These help the mic from picking up harsh noises such as when you "pop" your "P's."

◊   MICROPHONE PROCESSOR
This helps you even out the audio, minimize the background noise and clean up the signal. You will get a "radio sound" without having to tinker with the levels.

◊   MIXER
This box will give you control over the levels, inputs, outputs, etc. Such as making sure your voice is on the same level as a guest voice or piece of music etc.

◊   HEADPHONES
These allow you to have complete control over monitoring the audio. Earbuds can work but they won't give you clear quality and aren't recommended.

◊   SOUNDPROOFING
This may sound obvious. But adding soundproofing will eliminate extraneous noise and echo.

THE ART OF THE TALK

HOW TO TALK: IT'S EASIER SAID THAN DONE

Your voice is your tool, your money maker. Don't assume you can simply turn on the microphone and speak consistently without practice and purpose. Think about the following:

FLOW AND BREVITY:

Depending on the format, flow as we define it is the consistency of speech; brevity is the amount of time for which you must speak. Both utilize the following:

1. PROJECTION
    You don't want to scream at the audience. Don't mistake being energetic for being loud. But having said that, both being energetic and quiet can evoke different moods. What are you trying to say? Let the content guide your projection.

    a. ARTICULATION/CADENCE
        Be clear. The audience only hears you once. Do not mumble. Do not race through your words. You may be excited but remember your pacing and slow down.

        Be careful of something I call "tongue in teeth"—whereby you mush your words because you are pushing your tongue into your teeth and not allowing for articulation.

        Also, certainly, when starting, you may want to script or bullet point what you are going to say so that you are not fumbling for thoughts, and you can concentrate on speaking clearly.

b. INFLECTION

- Knowing when to highlight words and phrases can color a story or commentary nicely. You will want to emphasize when possible to make a point or clarify an issue. Use inflection. Again, this does not mean projection. Inflection is to change the tone or pitch of the voice only. In the end, you will create greater insight into your segment. Remember you are painting a picture with your words.

2. FILLER WORDS
"Um" "Ah" "So" and "Like" … are all filler words that are used as a crutch. They are the words that fill the empty spaces when you are thinking about what you are going to say next. How do you identify them? Start listening back to your air check. They will begin to annoy even you. The only way to get rid of them is to practice...AND...to slow down just long enough to collect your thoughts so you are not fumbling with empty spaces. Again, bullet point ideas so you are not grappling with what to say next. Eventually, you will talk yourself out of them.

3. THE AUDIENCE OF ONE
You have to entertain yourself. You are alone, in a room, talking in a void. It is not as easy as it sounds. It is very easy to lose energy, focus, the sight of an audience, and connectivity. So you have to remember that you are never alone. Here are some tips to not fall into a vortex of being alone:

- ◊ Use imagery—think of one person.

- ◊ Make a connection with one person as opposed

to talking to the collective, which can be over-whelming. And if you convince the individual you are connecting to them personally, they feel more loyal.

◊   Open the cell phone and turn the camera to yourself and talk. It reminds you of pace and a conversational tone by seeing yourself in the mirror. Of course, you could use an old-fash-ioned mirror!

4.   WHAT IF IT'S YOU BEING INTERVIEWED?
Not everyone wants to be a host or presenter. That doesn't mean you may not find yourself in front of the microphone. Should you find yourself as an interviewee on a radio and this can occur for any number of reasons these days. You could be promoting a product or service, brand, or business. Besides knowing how long the interview is, the following should keep you engaging and on point:

PREPARE FOR AN ABRUPT START
Simply put, be ready. The studio is ongoing. You are generally walking into a working program and there won't be enough time for getting to know you. When you sit down, it's "go" time.

SHOW PASSION AND ENTHUSIASM
But don't overdo it. Relax. You do want to promote what you are there for. Confidence is key. Be someone you want to listen to...no one wants to be bored.

BE CLOSE TO THE MIC
You want to be heard. There may not be time for a mic sound check. So stay close to get the best sound quality.

CONNECT WITH HOST
You want to have a cordial conversation with the host. But
don't let the mood of the host deter you from delivering your
message. Make sure if the questions are off your point, you
bring them back around. Remember, there is nothing in it for
the host to promote your product or message. It is up to you.

MAKE THE PLUG—DON'T WAIT FOR THEM TO DO IT
Generally, the conversation will fly by. You want to make sure
you get your point across and it is not lost in miscellaneous
conversation.

TREAT CRAZY CALLERS WITH RESPECT
You never know who can call in. You don't want to be hostile
or irreverent as a guest. Be a great representation of your
brand.

DON'T GIVE LONG ANSWERS
You don't want to use up all your time on one or two questions. AND do not give yes or no answers.

DON'T BE COMPLEX
Don't confuse the audience with facts and figures that take a
long explanation or can't be explained at all. Be familiar with
the audience. You might as well be speaking a different language. You must connect with the audience. You don't want
to speak above or beneath the audience.

DON'T BE ALARMIST
Don't scare the audience with false or incendiary information.

REMEMBER HUMOR WHEN APPROPRIATE
A pleasant person is always appreciated...and chances are,

invited back. If you are entertaining the audience, you have a
higher reason for being invited back to the show.

DIFFERENT KINDS OF PROGRAMMING

Radio program formats differ by country, regulation, and market. In
addition, formats change in popularity as time passes and technology
improves. Early radio equipment only allowed program material to
be broadcast in real-time, live broadcasting. As technology improved,
an increasing amount of broadcast programming used pre-recorded
material. A current trend is the automation of radio stations. Still,
programming falls into topics and genres. You may find your niche in
any of the following:

TALK

You may think you have something to say, but can you sustain your
opinion for several hours, daily and keep people interested? Music is
not your buffer. So many talk radio hosts rely on guests to break up
their programming. Generally, if you are looking to get into this type
of programming, you will need to be an expert, a pundit, a specialist, or a notable figure. Generally, talk radio revolves around politics,
social issues, or relationship topics.

- Improvisational skills are key. Callers will be firing from all
  directions no matter what the topic is and it is incumbent on
  you to keep the conversation going and on point.

- Most talk shows will have a call screener. So that caller that is
  not on topic, will not necessarily be pushed on the air.

- Define a personality. Are you the bombastic instigator? Are
  you the listener? You can define your audience by defining
  your personality.

SIDEBAR—DREW STEELE

Starting as a recording engineer creating small independent label projects in Fort Myers, Florida, you wouldn't think of DREW STEELE as now one of the most popular local Fox Network Radio conservative talk hosts. His early years were very successful as a pop music writer for such artists as Samantha Cole, Chris Kirkpatrick, Willa Ford, Trick Pony, John Michael Montgomery, and others. Although his lyrics had plenty to say, STEELE had much more to say it seemed when he was asked to bring his talents to Top 40 morning shows on radio...but that was an accident, not a career ambition.

Why radio when it was all going so well for you?
"Giving up the music industry was hard...the pressure to come up with the next hit, the next great thing. But radio was still a chance to be expressive. Radio has instant gratification. The funny thing was, I didn't have radio experience. I was doing a DJ gig in a club in 1988 and a friend came up to me and said I just fired the afternoon guy at his station. I want you to do it. I had no idea what I was doing...but somehow, I just did it.
I created a character where I brought in clips and sound bites that I could react to. I was like my partner, so I wasn't alone in the studio. I had something to work off of."

When did the transition to talk radio occur?
"After 9/11. My dad was driving into the city, and he saw the planes going into the towers. He was on the phone with me describing it all. He was crying. I thought I needed to do something more important. I never thought politics or anything like that."

What makes a good host?

"You have to be honest. Otherwise, the audience can see right through it. You can't be driven by malice or hate. You have to have convictions. Are people hearing my heart? I want to know why you disagree with me. I am looking for discord. I think we have lost the art of agreeing to disagree. I want to take you to the edge. But I never know what the edge is. But the bottom line is: you have to be a voice for people who don't have a voice."

How do you deal with callers who can be unexpected or aggressive?
"Every caller is valid. I want them to help me understand where they are coming from. After I hear the question, I always know the direction of where the conversation is going. The most important part of the interplay is listening."

Drew's tips for people who want to hit the airwaves and talk:

- ◊ *NEVER TALK DOWN TO A CALLER*
  Besides the fact that they are your bread and butter, you never know where they are coming from initially. Take a moment to learn or assess what the situation is with the caller and go from there.

- ◊ *ADMIT WHEN YOU ARE WRONG*
  Be honest. It goes to trustworthiness.

- ◊ *LET THE AUDIENCE KNOW WHEN YOU DON'T HAVE THE ANSWER*
  No one knows everything. And there may be times when you learn from a caller.

*◊ **CONVICTIONS BASED ON YOUR REAL LIFE ARE YOUR BEST ASSET***
Don't be afraid to share real-life anecdotes. They give you credibility. Especially with talk, the audience wants to know if your opinion is grounded in something.

*◊ **PERSONALITY WILL FOLLOW CONTENT***
Generally, it is the other way around. In talk radio, concern yourself with the content and then develop your personality. If you are trying to develop a character first, the content may be tainted, compromised, or lost.

GENRES

Radio talent tends to follow the specific genre they are most comfortable working within. Although radio stations tend to have a taste of all genres along the different day parts. So, there may be different opportunities at the radio station which allow for lateral movement once there. Don't rule out any opportunity early on. But clarify what you truly are looking to do.

- MUSIC

  This genre is more personality driven. The type of music will define the personality that hosts it in terms of tone and presentation and content. Think of the difference between presenters of country genres versus hip hop. What fits your style? Where do you fit?

  No matter what genre you work in, it is not just about knowing the music; you must know about the culture that surrounds it. Know the news and trends. Remember you must create content to sustain an audience. You don't want to offend the audience who just may know more about the genre than you do. Know what you are talking about before you hit the mic.

- NEWS
This is all about being a journalist. If you aren't, this isn't for you. Being a gossip is not a journalist. It is not opinion based. And for the record, entertainment journalist are still journalists. They follow the same standards, practices, and ethics as hard news journalists. Other than talk format, most news these days is an off-shoot of the television-based subject matter.

  a. National Public Radio (NPR)
     This is wide scope, educational, lifestyle, news, and story-driven programming. It is in essence not a genre but more of a network unto itself. It is funded by grants and contributions and has a strict set of program considerations. Many are run through colleges and universities and while there is a wide berth of creativity, the budgets for programming are limited.

TIME SLOTS

What are radio day parts?
The broadcast day is segmented into blocks known as RADIO DAY PARTS:

- MORNING DRIVE:
The morning segment at most stations starts at 5 am or 6 am. It lasts for about 3 or 4 hours ending at 9 am, 10 am, or 11 am. This is the most profitable time of the radio day. Think about it. It's because most people listen to the radio in the morn-

ing—turning on the radio during their morning routine or while stuck in morning traffic jams.

Morning radio hosts are usually the biggest stars at the station and their shows are the highest profile. The programming format is composed of a mix of interviews, links between songs, wake-up calls, prank calls, weather announcements, comedy bits, newscasts, phone-ins, traffic segments, giveaways, etc. with a potential high-end ratio of 60% speech and 40% music.

- MID-DAY:
The segment starts from 9 am to 11 am. It ends at 2 pm or 3 pm. Mid-day hosts take over the airwaves during this period when people are busy at work or passively perform such things as household chores. Music is the main programming during this slot. Talk radio stations may take this opportunity to broadcast lengthy features, talk panels, etc.

- AFTERNOON DRIVE
The second most popular day part of the radio broadcast is the afternoon drive. It starts at 3 pm and ends at 7 pm. Audience numbers soar again due to the evening commute.

- EVENINGS/OVERNIGHTS
Evenings start from 7 pm to 12 pm. Radios receive fewer tune-ins since people are either watching TV, streaming shows or sleeping. Many stations slot in syndicated programming during this segment as it is cheaper to deliver than to produce and absorb the cost of original programming. Overnights or if you prefer the more ominous name "graveyard" shift spans from 12 am to 5 am or 6 am.

SOLO VS TEAMS

You may find yourself working either as a solo act or with a co-host over the course of your career. The two situations are very different. While we have talked about what you need to do to keep focus and on-point with working solo, as a co-host, let's explore the differences:

HOW IT WORKS

Even in a team situation, there can be a designated host or a lead person who will guide the direction of the show. The co-host will defer to that direction in terms of timing and content. But the co-host will retain their personality and perspective which is what makes the mix work.

WHEN IT WORKS

The morning drive is when it works best. Why? The lively banter is the wake-up crew. The evenings are another opportunity for team programming because it can be more of a "party" format.

WHY IT WORKS

The conversation is the voice of the listener. In many cases, the talk reflects what is on the minds of the audience without having to have caller interaction. Similarly, chat between the co-hosts can be entertainment-driven, they can talk and debate the news of the day, trends, and pop culture.

The one thing you don't want to see happen is the homogenization of the team into one voice. The nuance of personality is key. Remember to keep the different defined personalities as individuals. It keeps the audience entertained and the show on its toes.

AND WHEN YOU GET THAT JOB:

MARKETING/SELF-PROMOTION:

It is important that you promote your new position. You want to max-imize your listenership and fan base—not just for the success of your new situation but for the future. I suggest that you create new pro-fessional accounts on all social media platforms independent of your personal profiles and the social media the station or job is already doing for you and promote the new profession you have. While there is an in-depth discussion on how to create social media in the "Social Media" segment of this book, start out thinking about the following:

- Create a name or use your radio name such as: "First Lady Niki."

- Come up with a logo, design, or thumbnail picture that can be used as the best representative of that "character."

- Create selfies and/or short videos to highlight what you are doing and keep posting.

The idea is to create marketing for the fans and audience that "let them in" on who you are to the amount you are comfortable with. The benefit is you can collect these followers and take them with you from job to job. The station will own any publicity, marketing, or promotion they would have done for you. So if you create some for yourself, you will be ahead of the game.

A FINAL THOUGHT:

You will end up taking the good with the bad. Marc has done it, Niki has done it...you will do it!

KEVIN HART VS. GARY SPEARS... FUNNY... NOT SO FUNNY

Over the course of your career, you should be so lucky as to have guests who are so much fun and entertaining, that you wish the interview would never end and they would never leave. Unfortunately, you inevitably will also get the opposite—people for whom you just can't wait to leave. I have had both and the latter has caused so much drama, it seemed to come out on the air. This is a story of both sides of the coin, with of all people, comedians—trained to be fun. Well, one was...despite his personal drama...and the other was just pure drama. And the joke was on me.

I was scheduled to interview Kevin Hart at a time when Kevin was beginning to bubble on the surface. He had just done a standup comedy special in town, and sat with me to promote some local standup appearances. We were having a good time, a consummate professional who could turn any question into a setup line for a good joke. The conversation was going well when he gets the phone call. Speculation was swirling at this time that he was going through a divorce from his wife and as these things go...it wasn't going well. He stepped outside the studio, and he seemed to be visibly upset about the conversation, pacing back and forth. And not trying to eavesdrop on the conversation, I could tell that his mood shifted. I was concerned that our conversation was going to die and that we would have to end what was a great and entertaining interview.

He returned to the studio and like flipping a light switch, he turned on the Kevin Hart he had been all along. Funny. Entertaining. Professional. He knew what he was there for, and had a job to do. He left his personal life at the door. And that could be why he is where he is today, and comedian Gary Spears isn't.

Gary Spears was a comedian I had been looking forward to interviewing as I was already a fan of his work. I had followed his work during his time on "MADD TV" and loved his very popular celebrity impersonations. So having a chance to sit down and talk with him was exciting! Or at least that was the expectation.

When the time arrived, there wasn't much time for a meet and greet before we were to go live but he was greeted warmly when he walked into the room. When I have guests, I like to create a conversation with our time together on the show rather than the obvious Q&A consisting of the commonly asked questions, routine guest answers, a plug, for what they are doing, etc. I conducted interviews this way, especially with comedians, so that our audience would have an opportunity to hear a different side of the star's story and not hear pre-planned jokes or jokes they would hear later on the stage. It is a comfortable approach, and the presumption is that any seasoned talent could flow well with this format. Spears is seasoned, I presumed, so let's have some fun.

The mic goes on, and we get started. But within only a couple of minutes, you could quickly tell the energy was shifting a bit. His answers were getting shorter and decidedly unfunny. It was decided to take a break and, when the microphone goes off, he asks the handler to step outside. What ensues outside in the hallway is a somewhat heated conversation—unfortunately out of earshot.

Once back and on the air, things go from bad to WOOOORSE. He was not only rude, but even the energy in the room also went stale and cold—so much so, it was decided to wrap the interview. From what we heard he had quite a few complaints about us and, needless to say, we had ours too! We subsequently found out, he was angry over the fact that we never used his pre-planned jokes. You know the jokes, the ones the audience at the comedy club would be paying to hear that night...again. I am However proud of myself for not having lost my cool with him on the air.

You see, there are some things that you'll never need to explain to your audience. If a person is an as***le, they'll come across as an as***le. The audience hears what you hear, and tweaks to what you are feeling. As long as you don't sink to their level, you will come across the better person—the professional. I like to think the difference between Kevin Hart, who left his drama in the hallway, and Gary Spears, who went out in the hallway to create drama to bring into the interview, is to just look at where the two have them are today.   One is an international star and the other is Gary Spears. I wonder how that happened. ,,

PODCAST

PODCAST

Adnan Syed is not guilty, but he isn't necessarily innocent either. But he shouldn't spend any more time in prison for a crime no one can figure out whether he committed. So after spending 23 years of a life sentence for the 1999 murder of Hae Min Lee, Baltimore City Circuit Judge Melissa Phinn vacated the sentence. How did this happen? Because of the interest in the case on the popular first series of SERIAL— a Peabody Award-winning, investigative journalism, true crime genre, podcast owned by the New York Times, hosted by Sarah Koenig and created by Julie Snyder. The podcast started to investigate Syed and his claim of innocence and that there was not enough evidence to convict beyond a reasonable doubt. The truth was, there wasn't... but his claim of an alibi could not be corroborated either. The podcast asked if either or could not be proven, how could Syed be in prison for life? And the question resonated enough to get Syed a new trial. Subsequently, Syed was released, and SERIAL became a sensation. By 2018 episodes of seasons 1 & 2 of its now 3 seasons, have been downloaded over 340 million times, establishing a podcast world record.

Herein lies the power of the podcast.

The multi-EMMY nominated television streaming dramedy ONLY MURDERS IN THE BUILDING, created by Steve Martin and John Hoffman and starring Martin, Martin Short, and Selena Gomez takes a comic approach to crime mystery fiction but with a twist. The main characters all share an interest in true crime podcasts and together set out to solve a murder in their tony New York apartment co-op to feed their podcast episodes. It's an entire television series about a podcast.

Herein lies the popularity of the podcast.

SO, YOU WANT TO CREATE A PODCAST!

There is an old saying that, more or less, states not everything is for everyone. Well, a podcast can be for anyone. Why not? It is easy to do, and easy to create...but as of 2022, there are over 2 million podcasts out there with close to 50 million podcast episodes. That is a deep pool to swim in. But to stand out, break out, sound out, shout out...you should know:

- 80% of listeners stay tuned for all or most of the episode.

- Some 90 million Americans (44% of the population) have listened to a podcast.

- Over 66% of listeners act based on the ads they hear on podcasts.

- The average podcast gets just over 140 downloads per episode.

- Over the past four years, podcast listening has grown 120% each week.

- Experts say by 2023 there will be 160 million listeners.

PART ONE:

WHAT IS A PODCAST?

In technical speak, a podcast is an audio file that's made available on the internet. Listeners can download the file to their devices or stream it through a listening app.

In simple speak, a podcast is much like subscription-based talk radio—a series of spoken audio episodes focusing on a particular theme or topic.

RADIO IN YOUR PAJAMAS FROM HOME!

For those looking to start a podcast, you should read the RADIO section of this book to get a clear understanding of the broadcast technique that best serves you as a podcaster as podcasting is, as best described, radio on the internet.

PODCASTING VS. BROADCAST RADIO

Doing a podcast can be fun! It's the opportunity to expound upon a topic, show off expertise or simply entertain. Podcasting is an extended conversation, generally without music as a buffer between segments. The only time limit you have is the one you set. These days, the popularity of podcasts has gotten some radio morning shows to repurpose the programming by taking their show, re-editing by cutting out the commercials and music, and calling it a podcast. And technically they are right. But, there are also those in broadcast radio that use the podcast format to have extended conversations about the topics already spoken about on their particular radio show—inviting you to extend the conversation.

And while some radio professionals are using podcasts as an adjunct to connect further with their audience and expand their influence, newcomers to the business are finding podcasting is their way in—finding and defining a voice when other opportunities have yet to present themselves.

So why get into the medium? There can be plenty of reasons—from personal to professional—but as you are effectively your own boss, producer, editorial content developer, and talent; it is yours to run with. So why not.

REASONS TO:

◊ YOU HAVE SOMETHING TO SAY, AND YOU WANT AN AUDIENCE
That is the basic premise of why you would want to do this. But be specific as to what your goals are and what you want to achieve. Focus is key in a vast pool of pod-casts. The more you can find your audience, home in on them, and build on them; the more successful you will be.

Take into consideration where you fall within the follow-ing categories before you build your podcast. The subject matter and content can evolve but it may be colored by the motivational lane within which you are driving.

◊ ARE YOU TRYING TO BUILD CREDIBILITY?
Do you have a product/service to offer which needs this medium to validate? Are you promoting a business or talent?

◊ NETWORKING WITH LIKE-MINDED INDIVIDUALS
Are you using this podcast as a forum for ideas?

◊ STORYTELLER
You can create entertainment with a podcast—much like radio theater or audiobooks.

◊ COMMENTARY
Are you a voice for political or social messaging?

◊ STREAM OF REVENUE
This can be a lucrative business venture. But it takes work, diligence, continued content, and networking on other platforms. The key is to be creatively individual and have a unique niche that the audience can count on for you, and only you, to deliver. We will explore revenue options a little later in this section of the book.

MISCONCEPTIONS:

- YOU DON'T NECESSARILY NEED TO BE AN EXPERT BUT YOU DO NEED SUSTAINABILITY AND CREDIBILITY
That isn't to say expertise isn't valued. But perhaps you present yourself as curious but knowledgeable on a subject matter. You become a sleuth for the answers. That can be your niche. But you have to have credibility in why you are asking the question, can find the answer, and want to know the answer... rather than present as a random participant. Even a tangential connection to the subject matter that you want to talk about will give you the credibility you need. Use it.

- IT DOESN'T HAVE TO BE EXPENSIVE

- YOU CAN START WITH ZERO DOLLARS BUT A MIC CAN COST AS LITTLE AS $20 AND AS MUCH AS $10,000
Research what you need to start the process in terms of equipment. Do not overspend. You can always upgrade as

necessary. Get into the game and your needs may change as your success grows.

- YOU DON'T HAVE TO BE A STAR TO START
  A lot of celebrities or "names" have established podcasts and, needless to say, have garnered instant followings. Again, it is a matter of creating unique niche content and being able to market it to a broad audience.

- LENGTH IS ARBITRARY
  You can create episodes as long as you like. The most popular length for listeners is approximately 20 minutes. You have to take into consideration that many of the audience is listening in transit or short bursts. You don't want to lose them. Also, should you want to do excerpts for other platforms, you will want easily editable sections.

SIDEBAR: MICHAEL CASTNER

Michael Castner is a journalist, television host, and radio personality—currently the morning national news anchor for NBC News Radio. Most recent radio credits include "THE MICHAEL CASTNER SHOW" on KEX, Portland, Oregon, and the syndicated "THE DAILY WRAP" for The Wall Street Journal Radio Network. His previous credits include stints with iHeart and Bonneville International radio stations across the country. But most notably, Castner made a name for himself on-camera as the 14-year host of his celebrity talk show and red carpet/event host for E! Network. Early on in his career, Castner served as the press advisor to congressional candidate Joseph P. Kennedy.

These days, Castner owns the moniker PodCastner through which he has developed several different incarnations of popular podcasts.

They were, by design, short-lived due to contractual obligations with his radio duties. Nonetheless, he is quick to point out the creative freedom that podcasting provides and fully encourages people with clear objectives to dive into the pool.

How did a podcast begin for you?
"I was doing a show called THE NIGHTSIDE PROJECT for Bonneville International and airing on KSL in Salt Lake City, KTAR in Phoenix, and WWWT in Washington. The show was very popular and was scheduled to go into syndication when it was suddenly canceled. I was left hanging without a job…but with an audience. So as simple as that, I set up a mic and makeshift studio in my home and started to broadcast what became THE MICHAEL CASTNER SHOW. I had 10,000 listeners and did 60 one-hour episodes."

Why stop?
"Radio came calling again. And I could not do both contractually."

But you have come back to podcasting?
"I have. I registered the name PodCastner and through that, I have developed another incarnation of THE MICHAEL CASTNER SHOW and, to date, have done 120 episodes of a talker. I have had guests such as former Secretary of Defense Donald Rumsfeld and political commentator David Gergen. Currently, PodCastner is on hiatus…again due to radio obligations. But I love it too much to walk away."

Understanding how radio and social media work closely with podcasting, here are Castner's five tips:

◊ *KEEP YOUR FOLLOWERS—FROM LOCAL RADIO*
*Should you have a following on local radio...
or on social media...make sure your followers
know and follow your podcast on a national
level. Exploit your existing fan base! Encourage them to spread the word and you exponentially will get more followers.*

◊ *PICK TOPICS FOR DISCUSSION THAT PEOPLE
CAN RELATE TO*
*Don't try to be too esoteric or "out there." If
you have guests, let them be the crazy opinion
that you can volley off of. But if you are too
far afield, you may not keep credibility or an
audience at all.*

◊ *TURN TO TWITTER (OR OTHER SOCIAL MEDIA)
TO FIND GUESTS*
*People on chat social media such as Twitter
have something to say. And want to say it!
Simply ask them if they would like them to be
a guest. It is a numbers game...and the numbers are in your favor.*

◊ *YOU ARE THE BRAND*
*Remember that you are creating a brand
and that product has value. Treat it as such.
Develop it, nurture it, and market it. And you
can take that brand to other media platforms
and hopefully turn it into profit. I refer often
to a character known as "BRU ON THE RADIO".
Simply look him up. It is exactly why Castner
developed PodCastner—it is brandable.*

◊   DON'T OVERTHINK:

    a.   THE SUBJECT MATTER
    Create a niche and develop it. The content will come if you don't be too narrow-focused. If your subject is Granny Smith apples, then you are being narrow-focused. If your subject is apples in general, you broaden your scope and can include Granny Smith apples.

    b.   THE COMPETITION
    There are many, many fish in the podcast sea. But if you are unique, there is only one you. Believe in that.

    c.   THE ODDS OF SUCCESS
    Success comes with work and commitment—not just clever content, personality, and uniqueness. This is no different from any other commitment, you get out of it what you put into it. You can worry about the odds of success because then you dwell on the certainty of failure.

PART TWO:

HOW DO YOU CREATE A PODCAST?

THE NUTS AND BOLTS OF HOW IT WORKS

EQUIPMENT AND COSTS

There is plenty of podcasting equipment out there. That doesn't mean you need it all, especially if you are just starting. You will need a microphone and a computer—those are essential.

- MICS
  You can easily research the different kinds of microphones. Do not rely on your computer mic. You will at least need a USB mic. Take into consideration, if you are going to have more than one speaker—either a co-host or routine guests— you are going to need multiple XLR mics and an audio inter- face or mixer hook-up. While we are not endorsing any one brand, the name that comes up often is Rode for mics. Again, the price can be just tens of dollars to thousands of dollars. What do you want to spend? More importantly, what do you need to spend? Start smart, start inexpensively. If the quality is not right, you can always move up.

  As you expand, you should think about pop screens, mic stands, headphones, etc., all of which can also be purchased in kit form.

- SOFTWARE

  Audacity and Garageband is the software for beginners. They're free and relatively easy to use. Again, if you are looking for an editing tutorial, this is the wrong book. There is plenty of YouTube and Google information waiting for you. Suffice it to say. If you are on a more professional level, Adobe Audition, Logic Pro X, Podcast Pro from Rode, and Hindenburg Journalist are available.

- EDITING

  Should you have no interest at all in editing, there are plenty of will freelancers out there at reasonable prices on websites like Facebook. Shop around

DEFINE A NICHE

- What are you going to talk about? Are you a comic? There are plenty of jokesters out there. And if you think you can come up with a comedy routine every week...good luck...the best of them can't. A good observational commentary on a subject matter from a comic point of view can work such as Life (Surviving) in Los Angeles, New York, or any other big city

  Similarly, if you are an expert on bicycles, do you have to talk about how a bicycle works or would it be better to talk about the places that you go, trips you can take, or profiles on bicyclists to flesh out your podcast?

  Finding your niche is a great start but creating a unique perspective on the subject matter is what is going to make you stand out. Don't think it begins and ends with "I am going to talk about (fill in the blank)." You have to develop the concept. Don't be afraid to let your creative juices flow. Remember you are not doing this to hear yourself speak. You are doing this for the audience to hear you speak. Entertain them.

DO YOUR RESEARCH

Once you find your niche, do your research. Is there a glut of similar podcasts therefore, the question is: how are you going to make yours unique? Is there enough content to sustain a long run of episodes, given that is the goal? Are you correct in your initial hypothesis in taking on the subject matter, to begin with? If you can think it up at this stage…ask it, then answer it. It will pay off.

FINDING CONTENT

Once your subject matter is solid, let's make sure you can find content on an ongoing basis.

1. HOW DO YOU FIND SUBJECT MATTER THAT MATTERS
    The internet is your friend. What are people talking about? What is newsworthy or trending? Do people care…that is the question you should be asking every time. And then follow that up with: WHY? Answer "why" on your podcast.

2. CAN IT BE TALKED ABOUT AND BUZZED ABOUT?
    Not the subject but your content! Did you present in an entertaining enough way to get people to come back for more and refer others? They would not have downloaded in the first place if the content wasn't of interest. They will not stay with you if you are not of interest.

3. IS IT TOO BROAD OR TOO LIMITED?
   Stay focused...but don't be myopic. Balance.
   Let examples and anecdotes do the fine punctuation. Think of the following as a good equation to follow.

   ZONE IN: BUSINESS = HOW TO OPEN
   A CANDY STORE

4. ARE YOU AN ACTUAL EXPERT OR
   AN OBSERVER?
   The difference is: are you going to explain in
   actual defining terms or are you going to comment on the subject as you see it? Both have
   value so much as they have a point of view.
   Define your point of view and stick to it, at least
   initially. The audience will want to know who
   you are and not have to guess who you are in
   this episode. Either case can be highly effective
   whether you are providing answers or asking a
   question and seeking answers. Again, find your
   voice.

5. WHO IS THE AUDIENCE?
   You will want to know who, ideally, you are
   trying to reach. Of course, the answer is the
   broadest possible audience. But let's start with
   a target demographic and market to them. You
   can always expand from there. For instance, if
   your podcast is about basketball, you will market to basketball fans, not baseball. But as you
   expand your popularity and reach you will market to sports fans in general. If your podcast is
   more focused, stay focused to start. You want
   to make sure the content connects, accepts

feedback, and hones accordingly. Then market
to the broadest possible audience. You may
have to broaden your content as you broaden
your audience.

WHAT'S IN NAME?

Everything! If your name doesn't resonate, it is lost. You will want to
name your podcast with something that the audience with grab onto,
remember, find clever, and can easily find randomly within the sea of
other podcasts and tweak to.

    a.   MEMORABLE
How do you make it memorable? Play on words. Is there
a brand it is associated with? Can you make a pun out of
it? Can you play off the host's name? Is there a play off
the content or subject matter? Give this some thought.

    b.   NAME EACH EPISODE
Just like you have given your podcast a clever name, give
each episode a clever name. Listeners can easily refer
back to them or refer them to others. You may want to
refer by title as well on other platforms when you are marketing or publicizing your podcasts. Overall, you want to
create a library of episodes. Think: Michael Caster owning
PODCASTNER.

CREATE ARTWORK

You will want to create a logo or similar artwork that represents you,
the name, or the content of the podcast to act as a thumbnail on
listing sights along with your name. You will also put it up on your
website.

BUILD YOUR BRAND

It is all about continuous marketing. I know that sounds like a full-time job. But start to schedule the build. Determine how many podcast episodes you are going to publish each month and determine when you are going to produce them. You can easily extract excerpts at the time of production and schedule those for TikTok or Facebook distribution during the time of podcast distribution. It is a matter of structure and planning. Think about multitasking on a multi-platform market, BOTH the podcast and yourself equally.

WHO ARE YOU AND WHY SHOULD WE CARE?
Making sure people know who you are is important. Again, you don't have to be a star, celebrity, influencer, or expert to be a podcaster but people do want to know who you are. So let them know. You got into this for a reason. Let them know what that reason was, what led you to the podcast, and what were your experiences—profession-ally and personally—got you here…those sorts of things along with a well-written biography or resume will pro-vide people with a comprehensive idea of who and why. Peppering as you go with more information only adds to the mystique. But after people know "who" and "why" … define "what". That is done by the following:

(Both of the following have been explored in the RADIO section of this book…feel free to refer back to the appro-priate sections)

a. DEFINE YOUR VOICE/EXPERTISE
    This is not just with content…but with trust and credibility.

    b. CREATE PERSONALITY
       Don't be afraid to express your personality in a
       big way. Be appropriate to the subject matter
       but certainly be expressive and use your voice.

CREATE A WEBSITE

You will need a website. This is not a luxury but a necessity. As we have discussed, this does not have to be a laborious process or expensive. Turn to companies such as WIX to build your own. But you will want to house your biography, personal updates, the library of podcasts, branding information, merchandise sales (see later), and other information as a hub for the podcast.

Similarly, you should set up profiles on all the social media platforms and cross-promote the podcast. Use excerpts and highlights when possible to guide people to the podcast. Again, these links can also rest on the website.

SET IT UP ON A MEDIA PLATFORM/HOST

- WHAT IS A HOST?
  Apple Podcasts, Spotify, and Google Podcasts are not Hosts. They are publishing services or listing services where people can find you. You will need to publish your podcast to be found in the broad sense. But you need to be hosted to be broadcast. A broadcast host is a place to store and distribute your audio files. They also provide the necessary tools such as analytics, web players, scheduling tools, and other features to make publishing and expanding easier.

- HOW DO I CHOOSE?
  Do your research. Are you a beginner, a brand, or an enterprise customer? Each level has a price to match. But moreover, there are other considerations—mostly technical—such

as ease of use, audio quality, storage options, customer service, etc.

- HOW MUCH IS IT GOING TO COST?
  You expect your hosting will cost anywhere between $5 and $50 a month. Pricing is not just about the company you choose but also how many episodes you produce and how many downloads you expect to get. Also, popularity will factor in. The more popular, the more expensive. Of course, if you are more popular you might not mind.

- POPULAR HOST PLATFORMS
  While not endorsing any of the following. The list will give you an indication of some of the more popular host platforms. Take a look at each and research what they have to offer you to fulfill your needs:

Buzzsprout	Captivate	Transistor
Castos	RSS.com	Podbean
Resonate	OmnyStudio	Podcast Blastoff
Zencast. fm	Acast	Pinecast
PodOmatic	ShoutEngine	Podigee

CREATE A BACKLOG OF EPISODES

Before you launch, I suggest you produce or create several episodes ahead of time. Why? I believe in hitting the ground running. If you are a hit...and we all believe that the whole reason for doing this is to be a success... then the audience will be hungry for content. Have it ready for them. Have 5-10 episodes ready to "drop" after the first airs so the fickle audience, having found you and liked you, can immediately come back for more. You don't want them to lose interest in you as fast as they found you. Once they are hooked, adhere to a reasonable publishing schedule.

- PUBLISHING SCHEDULE

It is worth creating a delivery schedule for episodes. Realizing you are essentially your own boss, you must maintain discipline. The audience is going to want content regularly. How much can you create...how much can you deliver? Making a realistic schedule and sticking to it is not just good for you but provides consistency for your audience. I suggest that if you can create more product that you are scheduled to deliver, you only publish what is on your schedule so that in case of emergency, you will have a backlog of products you can deliver. Take into consideration if your content is timely and needs to air by a certain date for whatever reason. The product should have a timeless shelf life, but if you are a commentator, for instance, and talking about topical subject matter, you can not hold the product forever as it will inevitably be stale.

- TIMINGS:
Think about how long an episode should be to be most effective and entertaining. Take into consideration, the audience does not have the time to necessarily linger indefinitely over an episode. To that end, could one subject be broken into two or more shorter episodes?

The following gives you the popularity percentages of timed podcast episodes. This should be a good indicator of how long your segments should be:

    ◊   LESS THAN 10 MINUTES (14%)

    ◊   10-20 MINUTES (15%)

    ◊   20-40 MINUTES (31%)

    ◊   40-60 MINUTES (22%)

    ◊   OVER 60 MINUTES (7%)

PROMOTE IT

HOW DO YOU GET FOLLOWERS?

1. SHARE YOUR PODCAST WITH FAMILY AND FRIENDS
    This may seem obvious but be aggressive in asking them to share with their family and friends and so on. Build a network. It is no different from retweeting a message on Twitter. You will be surprised at just how many people you know...and, subsequently, how many people they know.

2. POST ON EPISODES ON SOCIAL MEDIA
    Utilize other social media platforms to get the message out or even truncated versions or teaser versions of your podcasts for rebroadcast. Be aggressive with this sort of self-promotion or marketing. It is what gets the word out.

3. JOIN GROUPS
    Research podcast groups, fan groups, and subject matter groups and join.

4. CROSS-PROMOTE WITH OTHER CREATORS
    Followers beget followers. Be a friend, help a friend. If you are a fan of another podcast, reach out. If you have fans that have podcasts, reach out. It works.

5. OVERCAST ADS
    Overcast ads help you grow your podcast's audience by reaching passionate podcast listeners on their terms, natively, right in their podcast app. Your ads appear below the controls on the Now Playing screen and in the Add Podcast directory, reaching potential new listeners as they search for new podcasts. Tapping brings up all of your episodes, inviting listeners to subscribe with a single tap.

PART THREE:

HOW DO YOU MAKE MONEY?

The ability to generate income is largely about popularity, needless to say. And that is determined by listenership. Determining the difference between large and small listenership is somewhat arbitrary or a dynamic that is specific to the sponsor, marketer, brand, etc. If they see you are reaching a tight, specific, and target-appealing demographic—even if it is small—they will step up. Of course, a large audience is advantageous overall. Strive for that. But aggressive marketing and growing the audience can make a difference...make all difference. You have to put in the effort to make the returns. And it can happen. The following are simple suggestions to start on the money trail:

LARGE LISTENERSHIP

- ◊ SPONSORED ADS
  You are simply paid to read ad copy from a sponsor. It is not unlike what radio DJs do for local/national sponsors. A standard, but negotiable, the rate is approximate: $18 per 1000 listeners.

- ◊ COMMISSION FROM SPONSORED LINKS
  You can post sponsored links that take the listener to product websites or buyer sites. You can negotiate a commission for all sales attributed to a click from your podcast. And that can be substantial.

- ◊ ADVERTISING NETWORKS
  Connecting with advertising networks is tantamount to signing with an agent for your podcast which can help you align with brands and other opportunities which coordi-

nate with your podcast monetarily. You will have to do
your research as to which agencies let you pitch directly to
companies and which reach out on your behalf.

SMALL LISTENERSHIP

◊   SPEAKING ENGAGEMENTS/PUBLIC APPEARANCES
Even with modest amounts of listeners, a smart, unique,
niche podcast can generate interest for ancillary opportunities. Good speakers and entertaining speakers are
always in demand on the public speaking circuit. You can
always use your podcast as a calling card to agencies who
book such talent, apply to university lecture opportunities, and the like to further your income potential. You can
also use your podcast as a platform to create paid consul-
tancy, coaching, or tutorial sessions.

◊   MEMBERSHIPS
Create additional content you hold back which sits behind
a paywall.

◊   MERCHANDISING
Clever merchandising is just a matter of marketing. If your
podcast lends itself to a character, slogan, phrase, or another type of swag; you can easily merchandise it on your
website.

POPULAR PODCASTS

We have taken a look at a list of some of the most popular podcasts. We encourage you to jump on to Spotify or other like engines and shop around. What seems to be a trend is true crime and new pundits being the most popular. And as you will see, celebrities don't make the list.

1. THE DAN BONGINO SHOW—RIGHT-WING POLITICAL COMMENTATOR AND AUTHOR

2. WTF WITH MARC MARON—CONVERSATIONS WITH POP CULTURE AND NEWSMAKERS

3. MORBID: A TRUE CRIME PODCAST—SERIAL KILLER FASCI-NATION

4. RADIOLAB—DEEP QUESTIONS WITH JOURNALIST AN-SWERS

5. WAIT WAIT...DON'T TELL ME—REGULAR PANELISTS QUIZ GUESTS ON TIMELY NEWS ISSUES

6. UP FIRST—TOP THREE NEWS STORIES OF THE DAY

7. PLANET MONEY—ECONOMIC STORIES

8. THE BEN SHAPIRO SHOW—CONSERVATIVE POLITICAL COMMENTATOR

9. CALL HER DADDY—SEXUAL EMPOWERMENT

10. OFFICE LADIES—BEHIND THE SCENES OF "THE OFFICE"

11. SERIAL—INVESTIGATIVE JOURNALISM AND NON-FICTION STORYTELLING

12. POD SAVE AMERICA—LIBERAL PODCAST

13. MY FAVORITE MURDER—TRUE CRIME HOSTED BY COME-DIANS

14. STUFF YOU SHOULD KNOW—POP CULTURE AND ECLECTIC TOPICS

15. THIS AMERICAN LIFE—THEMATIC TOPICS HOSTED BY IRA GLASS

16. CRIME JUNKIE—COVERING THE CRIME BEAT

17. THE JOE ROGAN EXPERIENCE—INFLAMMATORY COMMENTARY

TOP EARNING PODCASTERS

Yes, there is money in podcasting...big money. Not to everyone, but certainly to a select few. The top five podcasters of 2022 earned $70 million and as of 2019 advertisers shelled out about $700 million in supporting podcasts. By 2023, ad revenue is expected to skyrocket to $3 billion. Just who are those with the multi-million dollar microphones?

1. JOE ROGAN--$30 MILLION—190 MILLION DOWNLOADS A MONTH
(He recently signed a $100 million deal with Spotify.)

2. KAREN KILGARIFF & GEORGIA HARDSTARK, "MY FAVORITE MURDER"--$15 MILLION—35 MILLION DOWNLOADS A MONTH

3. DAVE RAMSEY--$10 MILLION—13 MILLION LISTENERS WEEKLY

4. DAX SHEPARD "ARMCHAIR EXPERT"--$9 MILLION—20 MILLION MONTHLY, 4000 LIVE LISTENERS

5. BILL SIMMONS--$7 MILLION

FUN FACTS

- 49% of people listen to podcasts at home vs. 22% who listen in their cars. (Source: Nielsen)

- Comedy is considered the most common podcast genre. It serves to provide joy, relieve tension and improve mood. (Source: Statista)

- The number of podcasters surged from 850,000 to 2 million between 2021 and 2022. (Source: Musicoomph)

- Mobile phones are the most used device for listening with 79% of listening hours, with 15% on laptops and 6% on tablets. (Source: Statista)

- 41% of podcasts are published every 8-14 days but 31% of podcast episodes are published every 3-7 days. 2% occur monthly. (Source: Buzzsprout)

- Podcast listeners spend an average of 6 hours, and 39 minutes a week on podcasts. (Source: riverside. fm)

- At least once a month, 25% of adults aged 55 and above listen to podcasts. 40% of monthly listeners are younger than 55. Only about 29% of females listen to podcasts monthly. (Sources respectfully: Buzzsprout, Statista, Edison Research)

- 27% of podcasters in the United States have a college degree. (Source: Podcastinsights)

- Weekly, 28% of Americans listen to a podcast. (Source: pewresearch.org)

- 45% of podcasters earn more than $250,000 a year. (Source: Nealschaffer)

SOCIAL MEDIA

SOCIAL MEDIA

WHAT ARE YOU TRYING TO ACHIEVE?

Here's a scenario:

You have written a cookbook. So, you set up a website with pictures of dishes you have made, recipes you have created, videos of cooking instructions, and, most importantly, how to buy them. Great! But how do people find that website? Social media! You get the message out with tweets on Twitter—hinting at great recipes available and where to find them. You put up videos on Tik Tok and YouTube, post pictures on Instagram, and keep the word going on Facebook. Cross-promotion on social media drives followers to your website and that equals potential sales.

Many millions of people worldwide enjoy "playing" on social media. Whether it is to stay in contact with friends, family, or business contacts; forward along and share clever, creative, funny, or memorable moments of their lives; or pursue business or professional contacts and information; social media provides multiple outlets and multiple platforms for all tastes and pursuits. In today's fast-moving information and career-building world though, social media is not a luxury; it is a necessity and a tool. It can be used to exponentially move your message, build your brand, define your person or product, and achieve global recognition. Similarly, if misused, it can damage all of the aforementioned. When designing and developing a strategy to market a product, or person, or spread a message you want to treat social media as a business rather than a "plaything" or an "also ran" in the strategy of success. When used effectively, the results can be astounding, far-reaching, and potentially personally and professionally profitable. So have fun but be smart, be savvy, and be strategic. Because once something is on the internet, it is on there forever. You don't want to post today, what you may regret tomorrow. There are a lot of tomorrows ahead.

PART ONE:

WHAT DO YOU NEED TO GET STARTED?

The bottom line is you need a camera, lighting, and a way of editing. This can be as easy as using your smartphone and a ring light or you can upgrade to as sophisticated a setup as you would like. We have already discussed the equipment options in the TELEVISION section of the book and they work for this section as well. But don't overthink the need for equipment. Again, a top-of-the-line smartphone can work exceptionally well for most platform needs. Nonetheless, we have reiterated the TELEVISION information in italics below to remind you of your options:

CAMERA EQUIPMENT

DIFFERENT KINDS OF CAMERAS

Cameras are, quite frankly, a personal choice. Only you can decide what your needs are and how sophisticated a setup with which you are looking to equip yourself. The following are the three camera options you can expect to work with:

- *DSLR*

- *CAMCORDERS*

- *GO PRO*

In terms of brands, Canon consistently ranks high with several models making top ten lists. But your brand loyalty to say Sony or Nikon may make you more comfortable with their products. You have to look at the price—assuming you can start at just under $1000 for a camera outfit and go on to spending many thousands for more sophisticated *equipment—or decide by features that will dictate both brand and price.*

One thing to take into consideration with your camera choice is what you intend to do with it, and whether it will require additional equipment. Will that equipment need to interface with that camera? Such as using external microphones. Does the camera have an input for that? How big of a tripod do you need? Does your camera package must accommodate both your immediate and future needs. So, think ahead. Think big picture.

CELL PHONE

Fortunately, your smartphone is equipped with a rather sophisticated camera already. The phone has a built-in light, microphone, and stabilizer. Broadcast-quality television commercials and even feature films have been shot with iPhones. The smartphone has come a long way. Use it.

Given that a smartphone has its obvious limitations, the industry has created a plethora of accessories to make the process of production more professional. For the more advanced user, you will want to invest in accessories made specifically for the YouTube/Vlog community. Look into these options:

- *Selfie tripod/mount rig*
- *Ring light/shotgun lights*
- *External directional microphone/lavaliere microphones*

LIGHTING

Let's take a moment to take note of lighting as lighting can make or break your video. The viewer will notice the impact of good or correct lighting. Creative lighting can establish a mood, manipulate the time of day, pinpoint information or details, create an alternative reality, and establish three dimensions. Something as simple as a ring light surrounding your smartphone makes all the difference in the quality of the recording you make for YouTube. If you aspire to be a makeup influencer, for instance, you want that ring light to show your face in the best possible light. You get the idea. Close-up lighting is just one aspect. Lighting subject matter requires understanding the basics of lighting techniques.

The basic canon for designing a workable lighting design is called 3-point lighting. 3-point lighting uses three light sources to illuminate the subject matter, provide basic shape, three dimensions, and separates *the subject from the background. These three light sources are the KEY, FILL, and BACK lights.*

- *KEY light: This* is the dominant light source focusing on the subject—say an interview. Typically, the key light is at least twice as bright as the *side-fill light. In the typical 3-point design, the KEY light* is placed 45 degrees to the side of the subject and at a 45-degree angle above the subject.

- *FILL light: This* is placed on the opposite side of the interview or subject matter and at approximately the same height and angle as the key light.   But usually, the fill light is at least half as bright as the key light. This provides a dimension to the shading of the subject matter, rather than a harsh flat face on lighting design.

- *BACK light: This* is placed behind the subject, again at about a 45-degree angle above and behind the subject. The brightness of the *backlight can range in intensity from the level of the fill light to that of the key light, depending on the reflectivity of your subject—what are they wearing, is the subject dark or light, shiny or dull?*

In combination, these lights provide basic illumination of the subject. Through manipulation of the brightness of the key and fill lights shadowing is created which gives the illusion of 3 dimensions to the subject. The backlight then helps define the shape of the subject and separates it from the background.

You will want to explore an investment in a lighting kit when you are looking at your equipment budget.

EDITING

Again, if you are looking for a primer that will teach you how to edit your content into a finished content segment, you have picked up the wrong book. There are plenty of tutorials on the web that will teach you the steps from basic to advanced. But I am suggesting that having even basic editing skills are value added in today's marketplace. Many news reporters, especially in smaller television markets, are expected to shoot and edit their segments as well as appear on camera. But creating captivating, entertaining, attractive content doesn't happen on the fly. It is only enhanced by clever editing. No one is expecting you to be the next Steven Spielberg but a little creative contouring can only help.

Editing systems don't have to cost you a fortune. The following is a list of the top five free editing programs available:

iMovie
This is only for Mac users. It is for the beginner editor but is extremely user-friendly. The downside is that it has limited effects and only two channels of video.

OPENSHOT
It runs on Mac and Windows and is great for beginners. It has a reasonable number of effects but is a little clunky and can run slowly.

VN VIDEO EDITOR
This is run on an app and on Mac whereby you can start editing on the go on the app and airdrop the project to your computer and finish it there. There are a lot of effects.

KDENLIVE
This is more suited to the intermediate-level editor. This would be a more professional-level version than Openshot.

DAVINCI RESOLVE
This would be considered professional-level editing. It requires a newer computer with an updated operating system to handle its capacity.

The following are the best payment systems:

FINAL CUT PRO
Can edit 8k video. Has a $300 cost but has a 90-day free trial.
CYBERLINK POWERDIRECTOR 365
This features 3000 effects, edits 8k video, and has access to 6 million stock photos and music.

ADOBE PREMIER PRO
Can edit 8k and VR content. Is the most highly rated system. But is the most expensive at $55 a month which includes After Effects technology.

PART TWO:

WHAT IS THE POINT OF SOCIAL MEDIA?

Social media should be considered as a tool—a marketing tool—in the way an advertising agency would use everything from billboards to radio spots to television commercials to magazine ads to get the message out. Social media is getting your message out. If you want to be "social" on social media, create two accounts: one for personal contact and the other for business usage. In this section, we are talking about the business benefits of social media.

When you determine the value of one or more social media platforms for your business messaging (and more than likely, you will want to cross-promote on as many platforms as you can) remember your logo or signage, the username associated with that platform, the content generated, the quality of the content and the frequency and kind of use all reflect on your brand. Strong self-restraint, editorializing, and content control are advised if you want to be seen as a consistent and professional provider of brand content—which is inevitably how you make money. That isn't to say that your brand may lean toward an outrageous product or content by its nature. So be it. Just be true to the brand and be consistent with what your messaging is about with that brand to be the most effective use of social media.

THE PLATFORM OPTIONS:

The following explains how to create accounts on the various popular platforms...NOT...what to do on the platforms. That should be determined by the needs of your message, product, or brand. We will touch on that later.

INSTAGRAM

HOW DO I CREATE AN ACCOUNT?

◊ DOWNLOAD THE APP AND PROVIDE THE SIGNIFICANT INFORMATION
Most people will use this on their phones, so you will find the app easily accessible from the app store on your smartphone. It will require basic information for you to fill in and once done you have an account.

◊ PICK A USERNAME
This is particularly important. Is your username relating to you (the person), you (the business), or you (the product or brand)? You want to pick a name that is easily remembered by those you want to reach. Do not mix business with pleasure. If you want a personal Instagram account for your vacation pictures and parties with friends, create that separately from your business account. Remember, if your name is linked in any way with your business account and pictures posted on your personal Instagram account may damage your business reputation...DON'T POST THEM.

◊ INSTAGRAM NAME GENERATORS
Should you be having problems choosing a name, Instagram has a tool to help you called name generators:

1. It works simply by asking you a series of questions regarding the content of your account and will come up with name suggestions from which you can pick.

2. The SPEEDY PASSWORD feature uses your first and last name and adds some "fun" additional words or phrases to the end.

3. The USER BUDDY feature picks a letter the name it comes up with uses alliteration. Sometimes, clever alliteration or puns make a name easier to remember or help them stand out better.

4. The LOGJAM feature uses random options.

◊   PROFILE PICTURE
Again, your profile picture may be as important as your name. If it is you, does it need to be business-appropriate, casual, or fun? Does the picture need to be of the product or a brand logo?

◊   START TO POST

1. POSTING A VIDEO
If you are posting a picture, it is just a matter of a drag and drop. But posting a video—which can be more effective for your needs if you are using this platform for marketing—consider the following:

- IF POSTING TO YOUR PROFILE=60 SECS

- IF POSTING TO YOUR STORY=15 SECS

- LIVE POSTINGS CAN BE AN HOUR
These are suggested times. You can post longer videos but be judicious in terms of timings. It is called "insta" gram for a reason. Should you need to crop or edit down your video, it is an easy fix with the built-in edit mode on your smartphone. Isolate the best of your video and post it. On Instagram, less is more.

- HOW DO I MONETIZE
Do you want to make money? It is a numbers game.

FOLLOWERS:
You need followers. You hear of the bigger celebrities, stars, and influencers having millions of followers on Instagram. People want to know what they say and what they put on display. You have to work the platform—aggressively post to entice people to follow you. You want followers and they want you. You not only have to click to follow and ask to be followed but interact with the people you follow. Comment on what you see, react to new content, and stay in touch. They are more likely to follow you and tag you on to others. Also, see whom others are following. Interested people tend to follow each other.

It is not about how many people you follow—although that is the catalyst to gaining followers—but how many people follow you. If you create a phenomenon, followers can find you. But you have to build it before they come. When it comes to monetization, take a look at the following:

◊ YOU MUST HAVE A MINIMUM OF 10,000 FOLLOWERS TO START GETTING PAID...BUT ENGAGEMENT IS BIGGER THAN FOLLOWERS.
What does that mean? You must engage on the site...be active, keep posting, show initiative, and be entertaining. You will not only attract followers, but you can also, eventually, attract sponsorship opportunities.

◊ 1 MILLION VIEWS = APPROXIMATELY $2,500-15,000
That is the earning potential for a million views. But you

don't want to be a one-hit wonder if you are developing a brand. You want posts to garner large viewership and likes every time. Again, defining a brand will help people to know what to expect...then you can occasionally surprise them with something special.

◊   WHAT TO EXPECT:
If you put the effort out, you can earn money per post. This is a pay expectation:

- KARDASHIAN = $ 250,000 PER POST

- TOP TIER INFLUENCERS = $10,000 PER POST

- MID-TIER = $1-5,000 PER POST

◊   WHAT THE SITE OFFERS:

1. AFFILIATE COMMERCE PROGRAM
   This allows for the site to match you with a brand for which you will earn a commission for sales the brand generates through the app for advertising on your site.

2. BRANDED CONTENT MARKETPLACE.
   This is a more sophisticated system by which the site helps match brands to emerging influencers. You may not just make hard cash but benefit greatly in goods and services such as courtesy meals and hotel rooms, clothes, makeup, jewelry, etc.

3. IGTV
   This allows creators to run short ads on their sites. You can charge for allowing it to happen or negotiate percentage of sales from monies made from the ad. This privilege requires a

minimum of 10,000 followers.

4. SPONSORED POSTS
    The more popular you become, the more at-
    tractive you become to brands. They will want
    your followers to follow them. At that point,
    you can negotiate a fee for sponsored posts...in
    other words, getting paid to post their message.
    It is a matter of setting a price to sell your popu-
    larity. (The Kardashians make millions doing it.)

ALTERNATIVE SITES:
There are other sites beyond Instagram which offer similar opportunities. Check out these:

- ELLO
  This is primarily interested in pop culture contributors.

- EYEEM
  This provides royalty-free photography.

FACEBOOK REELS

A Facebook account is easy enough to create. Keeping a Facebook
page is necessary to keep ongoing updates and postings with followers. But Facebook Reels is a separate function. You must be 18 years
old to participate. Facebook Reels are 60-second videos available for
creators to launch on the Facebook website in the following territo-
ries: U.S., Canada, India, and Mexico. You must adhere to Facebook
community standards. Another important piece of information you
should know is that you cannot launch or upload Reels from a computer. You must use your smartphone.

HOW DO I CREATE AN ACCOUNT?

- HAVE THE LATEST VERSION OF THE APP

- ON PERSONAL PROFILE:

    ◊ SELECT THE "REEL" BUTTON UNDER THE "MENU" BUTTON
    You can record live or choose from videos stored in the
    lists on the bottom left.

    ◊ EDITING
    Should you need to edit the length, for instance, select the
    length button and follow the easy options.

    ◊ FINISHED
    After your video is done, select "NEXT" and you will be
    prompted to write a description and add no more than
    four hashtags.

    ◊ SHARE THE REEL

- ON PAGES

    ◊ SELECT THE "REEL" BUTTON AFTER SELECTING
    "OVERVIEW"
    Follow accordingly.

HOW DO YOU MONETIZE?

- THIS IS AN INVITATION OPPORTUNITY ONLY:
  You are invited to the REELS PLAY BONUS PROGRAM and have
  to be invited again every month depending on your productivity.

- WHAT IS THE MEASURE OF PRODUCTIVITY?
  Videos must get at least 100 views over 30 days.

- PAYMENT:
  You get paid for reels on each of the platforms on which they
  are created. Bonuses begin at $100 for 1000 views. The maxi-

mum bonus is $35,000 a month. But you start at zero each month.

GOING VIRAL:

- INSPIRED BY TIKTOK
  The inspiration for REELS was TIKTOK. Facebook is making a run for that audience. Take what we have learned from TIK TOK and incorporate it on REELS. For instance:

  ◊ TRENDING SOUNDS ON TIKTOK
    One thing we have learned on TIKTOK is that certain sounds draw attention. What are they? Use them in your REELS video.

  ◊ USE INFORMATION VIEWERS NEED TO HEAR OR SEE OVER AGAIN
    Do not be a one-hit wonder. You have a message or product to promote...DO IT! Then do it again...and again. It is up to you to come up with clever ways to be entertaining without seeming redundant.

  ◊ POST OFTEN
    In the world of real estate, there are only three words: Location, Location, Location. In the world of Internet video production, we have some words for you: Volume, Volume, Volume...Content, Content, Content...Frequency, Frequency, Frequency... Consistency, Consistency, Consistency!

ALTERNATIVE SITES:
Should you simply be looking for an alternative to the Facebook site, the following are looking for you:

  ◊ MEWE
    The value of this site is there is no commercialization.

- ◊ NEXTDOOR

  This site narrows down your neighborhood and creates
  group chats among your neighbors.

- ◊ SIGNAL

  This site acts like Facebook Messenger.

- ◊ TELEGRAM

  This is a WhatsApp alternative.

- ◊ DIASPORA

  This site is very much designed to work like Facebook but
  has fewer functions.

TIKTOK

There are some 73 million TikTok users. And despite its controversies, it is a powerful communication tool in terms of short video distribution. Creating an account, like the others, begins as simply as downloading the app, signing on, and filling out the appropriate information. The difference is you must enter your birthday as you must be at least 13 years old to participate as a user. The more important information is knowing how to create a video:

HOW TO MAKE A VIDEO:

- To start: Tap the "+" symbol which allows you to use existing footage from the camera which you would have already captured or push the "RECORD" button to capture up to ten minutes of new footage.

  - ◊ You can adjust or edit the length of the clip by tapping the "ADJUST CLIPS" button on the right-hand menu.

  - ◊ Additionally, you can add music and sound effects by tapping the button at the top of the screen. There are sound effects available from TikTok. Do your research. Some sound effects attract more viewers than others. Find out which are the popular sounds and add them when appropriate.

◊ As you advance in your editing skills, other options include adding stickers, text, and effects. Play around and have fun. You can always erase mistakes or try again before posting.

◊ Once done, tap "NEXT" which allows you to add hashtags and:

- ALLOW DUET—Let other users create a split screen with their video.

- ALLOW STITCH—Let other viewers clip segments from your video.

- SELECT COVER—Select a still image from your video which acts as a thumbnail picture for your feed identification.

◊ After those final decisions, hit "POST" and you are done.

OTHER OPTIONS:

You have the option to make videos with multiple clips (up to 35 individual clips) by selecting a video from your camera roll or library.

- "ADJUST CLIP" allows you to adjust or manipulate the length and placement of each clip in the sequence.

- When it comes to the soundtrack, you can default to the original sound on the clip, and add music, sound effects, and voice-over. Placing soundtracks is no different than placing video clips. It is the same process. Regulate the sound level with the noise reducer.

- Additionally, you can add still pictures by selecting the photo option and adding up to 35 photos. Please note: You must choose them in order of appearance as you can't rearrange them in the same way you can the video clips.

    ◊ "VIDEO MODE" will play them in order.   "PHOTO MODE" allows you to toggle between them.

    ◊ SCHEDULING:

    ◊ If you are not ready to post your newly created video but you wish to release the video at a later date, follow accordingly:

    ◊ When you create your video, do not push "POST". Tap "NEXT" and then "MORE OPTIONS". Following that, tap "SAVE TO DEVICE." You can then preview your video before selecting "SCHEDULE FOR LATER." At that point, you can manually pick a publication date or pick from the three times that will be chosen for you.

TIPS YOU SHOULD KNOW

- USE TRENDING MUSIC AND SOUND EFFECTS
  They attract viewers. Getting viewers is the end game.

- THE FIRST THREE SECONDS ARE THE MOST IMPORTANT
  TikTok viewers are fickle. If you don't grab them in the first few seconds, you have lost them.

- HASHTAGS ARE KEY
  With tens of millions of videos in content distribution, hashtags let the viewer narrow the search. USE THEM!

- KEEP GOING WITH CONTENT

One-hit wonders are a rarity. If you are trying to brand a product, person, message, etc.; keep the content coming. If viewers have found you and you are getting "likes", they will come
back for more. So, give them more.

- TOO PROFESSIONAL IS OFF PUTTING...HAVE FUN
  No one is expecting Steven Spielberg...nor do they want him.
  They are looking for clever and quirky—something that will
  grab their attention. If it is too polished, it comes across as a
  commercial. Again, have fun.

- LESS IS MORE
  Sure, you can have a 10-minute video. And what you are
  trying to present may warrant it. But just remember, TikTok
  is a "hit and run" type of site. The most popular videos run
  between 7-15 seconds.

HOW DO YOU MONETIZE?

First, keep your expectations in check. Think of this as more of a
showcase than a place to become a millionaire. That isn't to say there
isn't an opportunity. But the goal should be about what you are putting out, not what you expect to take in.

- TIKTOK CREATOR FUND
  It is a suite of tools that allows users that are at least 18 years
  old with at least 10,000 followers to monetize:

  ◊ You must be based in the United States, Spain, the U.K.,
    France, Germany, or Italy.

  ◊ Along with 10,000 followers, you must have had 100,000
    views in the 30 days before applying.

  ◊ You must meet community standards and guidelines.

  ◊ Payment can be as low as 2-4 cents per 1000 views.

- VIRTUAL GIFTS
  This is part of the TikTok "CREATIVE NEXT" function which rewards creative programming.   The pay system is tiered and goes accordingly:

  ◊ COINS:
  This is app currency for viewers to buy gifts for creators.

  ◊ GIFTS:
  Gifts can be given to video creators with over 100,000 followers and to live creators with 1000 followers. Based on the coin value of the gift, coins are traded up for Diamonds.

  ◊ DIAMONDS:
  Gifts collected by creators can be traded up for Diamonds which are redeemed for actual money. Each Diamond is worth about 5 cents.

- RECEIVE TIPS

  ◊ You must establish or set up a "STRIPE ACCOUNT" to process tips as they come in.

  ◊ Viewer tips max out at $100.

  ◊ Only personal TikTok accounts are eligible to accept tips… not business accounts.

UTILIZE TIKTOK CREATOR MARKETPLACE:
This tool helps facilitate the production of sponsored content— matching brands with content partners. To utilize this tool, you will first need a minimum of 10,000 followers.

◊   SELF PROMOTE:
TikTok is an excellent vehicle to self-promote. Use it.
What are you trying to sell? Your video may not be about
making money off the video views but rather making
money off the sales the video generates. Are you promoting such things as the following:

- NEW MUSIC
  Create a music video.

- BOOKS
  Read excerpts.

- SERVICES

- Display what you can do/offer/teach/train.

- Trafficking the video to other websites and
  cross-promoting is a natural progression for
  your video. Solicit others to rebroadcast. This
  is your opportunity to be shameless and un-
  apologetic. Take it.

◊   PROMOTE A SERVICE
Just to touch on services in a more in-depth way. The following shows three ways one video can offer four different services:

- COOKING A RECIPE: What are you offering?
  - Cooking classes
  - Restaurant reviews
  - Cookbook sales
  - Solicit to become a personal chef

Don't be afraid to cross-promote your options even on the
site with the same video. Clever marketing is just that...

clever marketing.

ALTERNATIVE SITES:
> o   STEEMIT
> This is a creative outlet for authors.

TWITTER (X)

Despite its news making headlines with its fluctuating format and image, Twitter (X), and media like it (Threads) is a communications phenomenon. For the sake of simplicity, I will continue this segment to refer to the media platform as Twitter. "Tweeting" is now part of the social vernacular. According to Omnicore, as of the start of 2022, Twitter had just over 200 million monetizable daily active users which created over half a billion daily tweets. Some fun facts include:

◊   23% of American adults use Twitter.

◊   46% report using Twitter daily…spending 6 minutes a day.

◊   Most of the Twitter audience is between 25-34 years old.

◊   27% of Twitter users are from urban areas.

◊   33% of Twitter users have a college degree.

◊   34% of Twitter users earn $75,000+ while 29% earn between $30-49,999.

◊   69% of Twitter users say they get news on the site.

◊   The average person has 707 followers.

◊   Twitter users are more likely to be Democrats than Republicans.

Remember, when you are tweeting, you have a limited number of characters to make your point, say your say, sell your message. Be clever and creative. Be careful with incendiary or accusatory attack speech. There are monitors and censors. You will quickly learn the very definition of "less is more."

HOW DO I CREATE AN ACCOUNT?

◊ You will want to go through this process on both your computer and your phone. Like with all apps, log on and click "SIGN UP." Fill in the appropriate information and click "NEXT."

◊ You will need to create a secure password.

◊ Click the topics that interest you and people you would like to follow. In this way, the site can narrow the millions of options that can be fed your way. You can skip this step for now. And there is always the search option once you are up and running.

◊ Pick a username or "handle" that makes sense. Again, is this a personal account or a business brand?

HOW DO I MONETIZE?

◊ CREATE A KILLER PROFILE
Followers will want to know who you are. Let them know...in a big way. Be colorful, be creative, but be correct. People can fact-check easily enough. You want to attract business sponsors by being dynamic and a standout.

◊ GROW YOUR FOLLOWERS
Followers beget followers. Like Instagram, you want to follow to be followed.

◊ Follow people relevant to your industry/target audience.

They will most likely tweet back and/or retweet your message.

    ◊ Add your Twitter handle to your email signature. People can reach out to you instantly.

    ◊ Promote your Twitter profile on other social media platforms. Again, cross-promotion is key to reaching the widest possible audience.

    ◊ Embed your Twitter feed to your website. You want a direct link from your website for instant communication activation.

◊ SPONSORED TWEETS

Should you amass enough followers, brands may pay you to tweet their information under your "handle." Look for and research like brands and solicit their participation.

    ◊ Prices range from $1-10,000 per tweet depending on the influencer.

◊ AFFILIATE MARKETING

You promote other users' products/services and receive a commission when your followers purchase off the link on your tweet. Some sites match Twitter users with those looking for affiliate marketing:

    ◊ SHARE-A-SALE

    ◊ AMAZON ASSOCIATES

    ◊ FLEXOFFERS

    ◊ CLICKBANK

But within AFFILIATE MARKETING, make sure you are staying with a niche that works for you. If you are known for food tweets, stick with food products to endorse.

◊   PROMOTE YOUR PRODUCTS:
Twitter users shopped online 6.9 times a month, while non-users shopped online just 4.3 times a month. Twitter users planned to spend 21.7% more than non-users in 6 months. Harness those shoppers.

◊   DRIVE TRAFFIC TO YOUR WEBSITE

◊   PROMOTE A GIVEAWAY
RAFFLEPRESS is a plug-in that can help you facilitate this process.

◊   CREATE TWITTER ADS
TWITTER MEDIA STUDIO lets you place in-stream video ads and in-stream video sponsorships right into your brand-safe Twitter video content so that you can earn money directly from the platform. The following are elements of the STUDIO that keep your production organized and efficient:

- Producer – Broadcast professional live streams, promote and schedule live streams, and create instant highlights of your stream with LiveCut.

- Library – Manage all of your videos, images, and GIFs in one place. You can also add user roles and permissions across your team.

- Analytics – Measure your performance on Twitter by viewing metrics of your tweets and earnings from monetized videos.

ALTERNATIVE SITES:

- ◊ PLURK
  This site is the most like Twitter.

- ◊ PEEKS SOCIAL
  This site is like Twitter but focuses on videos.

- ◊ AMINO
  This is site is attractive to teens.

- ◊ MASTODON
  This site is ideal if you are looking to make your social network.

- ◊ MINDS
  This site appeals to social influencers.

- ◊ AETHER
  This site leans toward Democratic voices.

POPULARITY WANES

It's true. Paris Hilton was the queen of all media until there was Kim Kardashian. Who is next? Could it be you? The point is: you have to work in the media. You can't stay on top without feeding the beast. And the media is a hungry beast. You must stay on top of trends and news. You must find a niche and create a buzz. While we have talked about how to get on and maintain being on the top platforms, you must remember they are symbiotic, feed off each other, and help each other. Cover the spectrum and cross-promote to maintain your exposure.

Remember the cookbook example from the beginning of this section?

When selling a product, you don't want to lose momentum. While it is all about you and the product initially, as we have discussed, you might want to introduce cross-promotions with other followers or brands to expand your audience. Remember, it is always about growth. If you are starting to stagnate in your audience or follower count…it's time to rethink your strategy for expansion. The good thing about these platforms is that they allow for limitless creativity.

PART THREE:

We have separated this specific platform because of its value in terms of being a multi-purpose vehicle for everything from pure entertainment to business marketing, to artistic expression, to brand building. YouTube. Its digital video format allows for short and longer messaging to reach a worldwide audience. You control the narrative. You control the content—within the standards of decency. There are 50 million users and 720,000 hours of product uploaded every day. USE IT!

WHAT DO YOU WANT TO SAY?

Are you an actor looking to show your talents to casting directors? Are you a wannabe chef looking to promote your skills to potential employers? Are you a comedian looking to broaden your fan base with new material? Are you a corporate spokesperson trying to message out the value of your company to investors? Are you a job recruiter looking for potential employees? Are you a social commentator or influencer looking to spread your opinions to the largest potential audience? YouTube can achieve all this for you. The trick is to not be random among 50 million users. Set up a YouTube channel that is uniquely your own and draws viewers to it. Make sure your content is consistent, captivating, on point, and entertaining. Viewers have short attention spans. Grab them and keep them.

- ◊   LESS IS MORE IN TERMS OF LENGTH

    - ◊   Be as long as it needs to be but as short as possible.

    - ◊   6-8 minutes is the ideal viewing time. A longer message might be better in a two-part video.

◊ Once you build trust, you can introduce a longer format video. The fans will stick around.

◊ QUIRKY IS BETTER THAN POLISHED IN TERMS OF STYLE

◊ THE FIRST FEW SECONDS IS WHEN YOU GRAB THEM...MAKE IT SOMETHING WORTH WATCHING

WHAT IS THE END GOAL?

We posed some questions as to why you may be on YouTube. But the end goal should be either to raise your personal or business profile or to generate profitability. And the two may not be the same.

I'll give you a secret about Hollywood and the entertainment business: Agents and managers can or will only do so much for you. Sure, they want a commission or percentage of your earnings but have they earned that commission? You must get out and market yourself. Whether you are an actor or an amateur, a professional or a novice, YouTube provides a platform like no other to exploit your skills. Agents and managers are using your YouTube projects to find you the work you could find on your own with smart marketing. The following are categories you may fall into and develop a channel accordingly:

- PERSONALITY
    - A SKILL OR TRADE
    - BRAND BUILDING
    - Think being the next Martha Stewart
    - COMMENTATOR
    - ACTOR/COMEDIAN

- BUSINESS
    - SELLING A PRODUCT LIKE A BOOK OR ALBUM
    - PROMOTING A BUSINESS

Once you build your channel and start providing content, it should lead you back somewhere. Make sure you have a clever website—a hub if you will—where contact information and/or sales information can easily be understood or gathered. This is all waste of time and effort if the viewer can't reach you to follow through if your end goal is to market or profit from the exercise.

HOW DO YOU BUILD A FOLLOWING?

◊ UNIQUENESS

I have said it before, and I will say it again. Not everyone can be a Kardashian but no one else can be you. What do you bring to the table that makes you unique? That is what you want to market and exploit.

I will tell you this example: People ask me all the time what I do for a living. And I tell them I sell brown shoes. They always wrinkle their noses or shrug their shoulders in disbelief because of course I am an entertainment developer, producer and author. But I insist on telling them I am selling brown shoes. And they insist on an explanation. So, I tell them, in the entertainment business everyone is wearing black shoes. But I am selling brown shoes. My job is not only to convince them that brown is the new black but I am the best person from whom to buy their new brown shoes.

With 720,000 hours of product going on YouTube every day, you too are selling brown shoes. So, what is it about you that gets people to buy your shoes?

Look at comedians for example. They come up with catch-phrases or beats or shtick that is uniquely their own. So, when you see them, you will see different jokes but you will see familiarity in the performance. Can you create familiarity in your presentation that creates comfort for the viewer to come back for more?

◊   CROSS-PROMOTE
I can't emphasize enough the value of cross-platform promotion to drive people to your YouTube channel. Do not assume your followers will grow organically. But be mindful, if you are going to place YouTube videos on Facebook Reels or Instagram or other platforms, those platforms use vertical video and YouTube allows for horizontal video. You will have to think of format options or editing when redistributing your video.

And again, have a landing spot—a well-designed website—which allows you to gather and create a library to collect your videos as well as direct the messaging in terms of biographical information, resumes, blogging, fan feedback, merchandising, etc.

LET'S TALK ABOUT SUCCESS: BRIAN ROBBINS

"HEAD OF THE CLASS"—the ABC network teen classroom comedy was a television hit and made a star out of Brian Robbins who played the role of Eric Mardian. So many young actors burn out...or worse. Not Robbins, who is now one of Hollywood's heads of the class. And how did he get there? Well, a big part of it was YouTube!

While Robbins went on to other acting and hosting gigs, he earned his chops as a producer with such shows as "SMALLVILLE" and "ONE TREE HILL." With a decade of success under his belt as an executive producer, many would assume Robbins could write his ticket in Hollywood. He turned his attention to something no one would expect: YouTube, where he created a channel called AwesomenessTV aimed at the teen audience. Under that umbrella, it created a sketch/music series of the same name which became a phenomenon, and the network grew to include teen dramas, live events, and more. The network was compared to a YouTube version of MTV. In 2013, AwesomenessTV was acquired by Dreamworks providing Robbins a payout in the tens of millions of dollars.

Through a series of acquisitions, Awesomeness TV is now the property of Paramount Worldwide and was once valued at $650 million. As for Robbins, he has gone from success to success. After stepping down from ATV, he subsequently landed at Nickelodeon and now is comfortably situated as the President and CEO of Paramount Pictures and Nickelodeon. He also serves as Chief Content Officer, Kids & Family at Paramount+. If you don't think YouTube matters. Ask Brian Robbins how he is doing.

SO, LET'S GET STARTED:
HOW DO I SET UP A YouTube CHANNEL?

FIRST SET UP AN ACCOUNT

- GO TO YOUTUBE
  This a computer-based process while other platforms are done over your smartphone. Click "SIGN IN" followed by "CREATE AN ACCOUNT."

  a. CHOOSE "FOR MYSELF" OR "TO MANAGE MY BUSINESS"
     This is important because it helps you distinguish your content. You can have more than one account. For instance: should you have a book to sell and you want that to be under your business account on which you can do selective readings and book-related marketing. But on your personal page, you want to market the author separately. That is fine.

     ◊ TIP: Go to the Channel Settings and add keywords that are relevant to your different accounts. It helps potential viewers find you in their search for things they may want to view. ONCE YOU HAVE AN ACCOUNT CLICK YOUR PROFILE PICTURE AND CLICK "CREATE A CHANNEL"

HOW DO I UPLOAD A VIDEO?

IF YOU ARE UPLOADING ON THE PHONE

- ◊ DOWNLOAD THE APP ON YOUR PHONE
  Tap your picture and Tap your channel.

  ◊ TAP THE CAMERA ICON AND FOLLOW ACCORDINGLY:
    You can record a new video, 'go live', or select a video from your library that you have already recorded.

1. You can record up to 15 minutes of the new video. But if you want to add longer videos, you must verify your account.

2. You can do some last-minute editing with the scissor icon and magic wand icon. iPhone and iPad have royalty-free music you can add as well. Tap "NEXT" when done.

3. Add a title of up to 100 characters long.

4. At this point, there is an option to add a description of your video. This will be relevant to people looking for your video or even randomly searching for videos like yours. If you are promoting something...TO ADD THE DETAILS!

1. SELECT VISIBILITY LEVEL:

   a. PRIVATE—Only visible when you are on-line.

   b. PUBLIC—Anyone can see your video.

   c. UNLISTED—Not publicly listed but anyone with the link can see the video

2. LOCATION CUE IS OPTIONAL
   This is an option as to whether you want to determine viewership by geography.

3. UPLOAD

   a. If you would like to add tags to make it easier for people to find your video, tap the three vertical dots and select "EDIT" and click "TAGS."

IF YOU ARE UPLOADING FROM A COMPUTER

LOG ON TO THE WEBSITE AND SIGN IN TO YOUR ACCOUNT

◊ Click the "CAMERA" icon with the "+" sign and click "UP-LOAD VIDEO."

◊ Drag and drop your video or click "SELECT VIDEO."

◊ Add the title and description.

◊ Click the thumbnail you want to use. This is a picture that will essentially be your cover art for your project in the library. Think of this as your album cover. Once you have decided on an image from your video, click "OPEN."

◊ You can now add your work to your playlist. This is an option. But if you do this, you must indicate...BY LAW...if your work is suitable for children under 13 years old.

◊ OPTIONS: (These are self-explanatory when you come to them.)

- PAID PROMOTIONS
- TAGS
- SUBTITLES-CLOSED CAPTIONING
- RECORDING DATE AND LOCATION
- CATEGORY
- COMMENTS AND RATINGS

◊ You can add end-of-screen cards to promote additional information regarding your video. This is optional. You may want to direct the viewer to your website for marketing purposes. Just a thought. Always remember the endgame.

◊   SELECT VISIBILITY OPTIONS (See above.)

◊   You have the option to schedule the launch of your video. This is a very important option as you may want to coordinate the distribution of your video with other marketing plans you have in the works.

◊   To do this, click "SAVE" or "SCHEDULE."

ARE THERE RESTRICTIONS?

You can't just put anything on YouTube. Pornography, for instance, is a no-go. And don't think you can say "Well, who defines porn?" The simple answer is YouTube does. To that end, there are two standards by which the producer must abide:

◊   PRODUCTION STANDARDS

◊   Music and copyrighted art must be licensed.

◊   Production can be horizontal in format.

◊   COMMUNITY STANDARDS
You can look online for the full details but these include:

◊   DECEPTIVE PRACTICES:
Scams
Fake media

◊   SENSITIVE CONTENT
Child safety
Pornography
Suicide or self-harm

◊   VIOLENT CONTENT
Cyberbullying

◊   REGULATED GOODS
    Firearms

◊   MISINFORMATION
    Political or social safety

HOW DO YOU MAKE MONEY?

NOTE: YOU NEED AT LEAST 4000 WATCHED HOURS IN THE PREVIOUS YEAR AND 1000 SUBSCRIBERS TO START EARN-ING MONEY

So how do you get there?

- ADD CONTENT:
    - ◊ Feed the beast. You can't expect viewers to check you out occasionally or randomly and consider that a success. You want followers. You must create

    - ◊ ongoing content to build a fan base. There are two things to consider:

        - Are you creating a channel with limited-run content? For example, a six-episode story arc or one book with limited readings. You want to market as such, so the viewer doesn't expect more than you are going to give.

        - Are you an ongoing 'act': comedian, chef, or influencer? Then you must think about sched-uling video drops so that the followers learn to expect something new from you are at regular intervals. Scheduling is a good way for you to not be overwhelmed with production or deliv-ery. Also, you may want to produce in advance, hold back content, and schedule releases later so that you are productively, ahead of the game.

    - ◊ Again, let me stress that the video should be as long as it needs to be but keep it as short as it can be. You don't

want to bore the viewer and expect them to come back
for more. If you have something that is going long and
could be broken into two or three shorter videos, do that.
Have them engaged for shorter periods, several times.
You will win in the long run.

◊   Remember to be of high quality but not too polished.
Quirky is what catches attention. If you think you are
James Cameron or Steven Spielberg...DON'T TRY IT HERE...
have some fun. Be professional...but think out of the box.
Creativity doesn't mean sloppy.

◊   Use those keywords and descriptors. They help potential
viewers find you. Don't be too abstract. But be on point.
Describe your videos in as much detail as possible. What
do you want the audience to look for let them know it is
here.

ENABLE MONETIZATION
This allows YouTube to put ads on your videos.

- SIGN UP WITH ADSENSE
  This allows you to create an account through which you can
  get paid.

- KEEP UP WITH YOUR ANALYTICS
  Click the "ANALYTICS" options in your Channel Menu. This
  keeps you up on earnings, ad performance, video views,
  demographics, and more. Yes, it is important to know if you
  are earning anything. And that is a big "IF", but the video
  views should be your interest. If you are not getting many,
  you should ask yourself whether it is the content, the performance, or the production style.

- CROSS-PROMOTE
  I will constantly remind you; this is a game of numbers. Remember that other platforms need other video formats when you drop them. But moreover, can you use the popularity of YouTube to drive your followers to your website where a deal can be done?

THE FOLLOWING IS A LIST OF YouTube SUCCESS STORIES:

I want to list a few of the aspirational current successful YouTubers. I encourage you to explore the site and find those you may relate to or are inspired by. But you can check these out as they are the most followed and most profitable people on the platform. What are they doing right? Is that what you are looking to do? What can you learn from the production, delivery, content, length, etc., to make your production stand out?

What do these have in common? They are simple and easily digestible. Your first lesson may be to not overcomplicate things. On the other hand, being clever and adding to production values can be captivating to a whole range of new viewers looking for more in-depth segments or content. Think of the success of Brian Robbins who created television series on YouTube not just segments.

TOP YOUTUBE CHANNELS

- MR. BEAST—182 MILLION SUBS
  He specializes in risk and stunt videos.

- PEWDIEPIE—111 MILLION SUBS
  Started as a gamer of live stream games and is now a pop culture commentator.

- KIDS DIANA SHOW—97.6 MILLION SUBS
  She is an 8-year-old phenomenon who along with her family makes role-play, music, and education videos.

- LIKE NATSYA—97.5 MILLION SUBS
  She is an 8-year-old from Russia who plays games with her dad.

- VLAD AND NIKI—83.6 MILLION SUBS
  Their vlogs are the 8th most viewed channel in the world, viewed in 21 languages and they earn $312,000 per video

TOP YOUTUBE EARNERS--FORBES

- JEFFEE STARR--$75 MILLION
  A singer and makeup artist has been able to turn YouTube popularity into a successful cosmetics line.

- RYAN KAJI--$32 MILLION
  This 9-year-old attracts viewers with science projects, skits, music videos, and more.

- RHETT & LINK--$17.5 MILLION EACH
  Comedy Duo/Intertainers.

- DANIEL MIDDLETON--$40 MILLION
  This professional gamer is the third richest in the world.

- EVAN FONG--$25 MILLION
  He is a video game commentator and music producer.

- MARKIPLIER--$28 MILLION
  He creates horror gameplay.

- PEWDIEPIE-$25 MILLION
  (See above)

- PRESTON ARSEMENT--$20 MIL
  He is both a gamer and a prankster.

- DUDE PERFECT-$20 MIL
  He creates multi-sports entertainment.

PART FOUR:

SO, YOU WANT TO BE AN INFLUENCER

This is the buzz term of the new millennium. Everyone thinks they can just get on the internet, model some shoes, talk about the steak they've just eaten at an upscale restaurant, put on makeup, or take a picture from a hotel room and they are an influencer. Wrong? It is not that simple. You have to work at collecting contacts, making content, getting followers, and most importantly having both something to say and a personality to deliver the information. We have touched on the basic points that define an influencer in the TELEVISION section of the book and we have reiterated in italics those points for you before we go on in greater detail:

WHAT IS AN INFLUENCER?

An Influencer is a popular or authority figure within an industry who shares opinions, knowledge, or advice. If you can think of it, you can be an influencer. But that doesn't mean you will gather followers or viewers... spread influence. It takes work to find your niche, consistency of content to gather a following, and personality and knowledge to keep interested.

   ◊   *THE DIFFERENT TYPES*
       Promotion is the principal idea behind influencing—either self (a skill, talent, trade, or advice) or a product.

   ◊   *NOT EVERYONE CAN BE A KARDASHIAN...*
       BUT NO ONE CAN BE YOU
       The immense popularity of certain celebrity influencers should not daunt you. Your contribution is uniquely your own. It is up to you to create and build your site to maximize its full potential.

◊ *DO YOU HAVE SOMETHING TO SAY*
It is as simple as having an interest, opinion, knowledge, and consistent content.

◊ *LESS IS MORE—DO ONE THING RIGHT*
Specialize: If your expertise is shoes, do not talk about ice cream. Similarly, if your expertise is 'pop culture' and a shoe is all the rage one day and an ice cream another then cover the spectrum under your greater umbrella. Remember you don't have to be an expert but you do have to be creditable.

◊ *HOW TO BECOME AN INFLUENCER?*
The hard part is becoming an influencer; it is the maintaining and growth of your site where the real work deems you an influencer. Still, you have to start, and the following is where it all begins:

FIND A NICHE AND DEVELOP A CONTENT STRATEGY
What is your expertise? Make sure you can create enough content to keep viewers clicking on and looking for more. Fans have a low attention span and will move on.

- *CHOOSE YOUR MEDIA PLATFORM*
  Where will you get the most exposure? TikTok, YouTube, Instagram...how about maintaining a presence on all platforms you can. It is essential.

MAINTAIN A WEBSITE
Create a website that can be a hub for all your information and direct followers to your different platforms. You don't have to hire a website company and spend thousands of dollars to do this. Simple drag-and-drop do-it-yourself web portals such as WIX will walk you through the process.

- *CREATE AN ENGAGING BIO—IMPRESS ME*
  *Who are you? Why should we listen to you?
  This is your chance to impress your audience.
  List interesting facts about yourself, why you
  are interested in the subject matter you are pur-
  ported to be an influencer on, and some educa-
  tional, work, or expertise experience.*

ENGAGE WITH YOUR AUDIENCE AND BE CONSISTENT
*Talk back with your viewers. Respond to their feedback.
Answer their questions. Be consistent with your posts.
Your viewers will be loyal to you if you are loyal to them.*

GROW YOUR NETWORK AND TRACK YOUR PROGRESS
You need to follow the business end of this process.

- *UNDERSTAND YOUR AUDIENCE*
  *Learn who your audience is to pinpoint demo-
  graphics that appeal to brand collaboration.*

- *ENGAGE BRANDS TO COLLABORATE*
  *Brands will come looking if you have what they
  need in terms of marketing value for their products.*

*STAY CURRENT, UP TO DATE, AND HAVE
A STRONG OPINION*
*Follow the trends, develop opinions and comments based
on facts, not rumors, and be current with information.*

TEACHER/INSTRUCTOR/SKILL PROMOTER
Are you simply taking to the airwaves because you have a specific skill you wish to publicize or popularize? The internet is a good home for you. If you are demonstrating a skill—such as a chef who is promoting a cookbook—or instructing a task—such as video editing—or doing online teaching—such as conducting a yoga class; the organization is key:

- *KNOW THE NUMBER OF STEPS YOUR TASK WILL TAKE*
  Count the steps of the process. Make sure you cover everything as the audience is seeing this for the first time. Break down those steps into easy visuals.

- *BE CLEAR AND CONCISE IN YOUR EXPLANATION*
  Explain everything clearly. Just like with the number of steps, you are explaining to an audience who has never heard the instructions before. You need to be clear and simplified, even if you think it is too simple. But there is a difference between being simple and clear and talking down to your viewer. Keep your energy high and remember to talk to the viewer and not at the viewer. You may want to practice several times before committing to recording.

- *MAKE SURE THE VISUALS MATCH THE TASK*
  Make sure what we are seeing is an example of what you are saying. Do not jump ahead or go backward. You may want to record once for visuals, once with an explanation, and once together and edit the finished product together to make sure you have covered all bases.

- *CAN YOU CONDENSE TIME?*
  Is this a long explanation? Or, does the process take time? Does something you are building need time to set or does a recipe need time to cook? If so you may want to make more than one product and have the finished piece ready to show rather than protract production.

- *IS THERE MORE THAN ONE EPISODE?*
  Are you creating enough of a library of episodes to keep the audience coming back?

ALL THAT BEING SAID...WHO ARE YOU?

The previous defines "what" you are...the following creates "who" you are. Creating a personality is important to gather followers. Are you trustworthy, engaging, personable, and easy to connect with? All of those aspects of "who" you are should be a part of crafting your social media presence. And they all have to relate to "what" you are doing on the various platforms. So:

ARE YOU SIMPLY POPULAR?
What makes you popular? Use it. Do you have opinions, knowledge, authority, or advice people will listen to...not what you think they will listen to...but conversation grounded in real information? That can be attractive to branding and marketing.

YOU DO NOT NEED TO BE FAMOUS
You do not have to be a celebrity or a "name." But you do need to create a following. And that takes work to become a "name." We have talked about everything from marketing and cross-promotion on different social platforms. But it still comes down to likeability. Can you create a defined persona—someone who provides a consistent delivery of information and entertainment? To do this it might be easy to script a format for your segments that include several "must include" bullet points every time.

Such as:
SHOULD YOU ENVISION YOURSELF AS A REVIEWER:

◊   INCLUDE TIME AND PLACE INFORMATION.

◊   INCLUDE WHY YOU CHOSE THE SUBJECT MATTER.

◊   INCLUDE YOUR REVIEW.

◊   PROVIDE A UNIQUELY CREATED PERSONAL "STAR RATING" …SO THAT PEOPLE LOOK TO YOU FOR YOUR RATE SCALE.

SHOULD YOU ENVISION YOURSELF AS A SOCIAL COMMENTATOR:

◊   PERHAPS COME UP WITH A CATCHY TITLE OR NAME FOR YOUR COMMENTARY: (For me it is: On The MARC).

◊   INCLUDE A SUBJECT INTRODUCTION: "Today it's all about…OR…Have you ever thought about…"

◊   INCLUDED WITH COMMENTARY IS A CLOSING THOUGHT FOR THE AUDIENCE/VIEWER/ FOLLOWER…SO THEY FEEL INCLUDED.

None of this is carved in stone. You must do what is right for you. But consistency or framework in delivery and information allows followers to better understand what they are in for.

INFLUENCER CATEGORIES:

Once you start gathering followers, you will fall into the following categories. These are what brand/marketing/advertising alliances are looking at in terms of investing in you.

- NANO-INFLUENCERS= 1-10,000 FOLLOWERS

- MICRO = 10-50,000 FOLLOWERS

- MID-TIER = 50-500,000 FOLLOWERS

- MACRO-INFLUENCERS = 500,000-1 MILLION FOLLOWER

- MEGA = OVER 1 MILLION FOLLOWERS

HOW TO:

FIND A NICHE

What are you good at? What do you know about it? What can you consistently talk about with authority?   Those are the first questions you should be asking once you have determined your format: reviewer, commentator, instructor, etc. Even if you think you have an original niche, do your research. Is the market saturated in the subject matter you believe you have "influence" within? Is there something like it or tangential that you can create that touches on what you initially thought you would create but can morph into some-thing new and uniquely yours? You have to be open-minded and fluid. The bottom line is: what makes you unique? If you can define your individuality within a subject matter and can create a "different" approach to delivering a message...you are on your way. Still, ask yourself:

- WHY DO PEOPLE WHAT TO HEAR WHAT YOU HAVE TO SAY?
  Remember passion can trump expertise.

- CAN YOU CONSTANTLY CREATE CONTENT?
  You must keep up with demand. Viewers/Followers will be voracious if you are popular and you need to constantly feed the beast. Does your subject matter allow for that? Do you have the resources and/or production capability to keep up with that?

OPTIMIZE SOCIAL MEDIA PLATFORMS

- YOU MAY WANT TO LOOK INTO BUSINESS ACCOUNTS ON THE MORE POPULAR SOCIAL PLATFORMS

- DEVELOP A WEBSITE AND HAVE A DYNAMIC BIO
  The bio is key. You want to explain your background in terms of qualifications for your influence authority. Be creative when you write...as creative as your segments. The biography of the person you are as well as your credentials. Also, have some great pictures done. You always want to present yourself in the best possible light. Provide life experiences as well as work experiences.

CULTIVATE YOUR AUDIENCE

- WHOM ARE YOU LOOKING TO REACH?
  Of course, you want to reach the broadest possible audience. But you initially want to reach the right audience. Do your research as to who is following segments like yours and perhaps adapt to their needs and wants. Target demographics are very attractive to marketers and branding opportunities.

- HOW ARE YOU DIFFERENT
  Constantly, research the competition. Make sure you are not falling into normalcy. You must always stand out as your own brand.

- ENGAGE WITH YOUR AUDIENCE
  If followers ask questions, answer them. If you are being followed, you may want to follow back on social platforms. Constructive criticism is just that, constructive. Listen to it. Collectively, this will remind the followers that you are one of them and not elitist and above them.

HOW DO YOU CREATE CONTENT?

First determine what you need, how often you need it, and what you need to do to produce it...then you can begin to create:

- WHAT IS YOUR CONTENT?
  Is it written such as blog posts or articles or video segments?

- DEVELOP YOUR VOICE
  Once you know what you need to create, determine your voice. Will you be informative or conversational? Chances are, your segments will be laced with opinions. Determine that opinion and stick with it: if you are a vegan, you are not going to review a steak house...OR...can you do a segment on vegan options when you find yourself with an impossible menu.   And finally, in developing your voice, always be authentic. People want to hear you. Give them that.

- BE CONSISTENT
  We have continued to talk about this. Make sure you are regularly dropping new content on several platforms. Know what you need for each and schedule appropriately. Try to bank content and release it in a well-planned release

  schedule. Research the various platforms as to which days get the best interest, the time of day that better drives the information, etc. Several platforms allow you to place your segments on the site but schedule the launch release time and date. This is helpful to know so that if you find out that Tuesdays at noon is the best time to drop a video—you can schedule that time and date for release without having to be online at the exact moment.
  BE RELEVANT
  Stay up to date with information, news, and trends. You don't want to post yesterday's information tomorrow. Social media

is so instantaneous these days, there is no time to waste. If you know a piece of information, it's a good bet you are not alone. Post it, post it, post it. You might not be first...but you will, at least, be on trend. The difference will be your presentation, voice, and opinion. And it is up to you to make that matter.

- GROW YOUR NETWORK
  Growth is everything. As we discussed your need to establish relationships with your followers, it is also important to establish solid relationships with other influences. You never know whom they know or what they hear. They can be a great deal of help in having their followers follow you.

  Similarly, you will want to meet industry experts. You want them to know what you can do for them, not the other way around. Inevitably, their interest in you will help you in the long run potentially in providing goods and services.

  And get off the web and into the crowd. Look for public speaking or appearance opportunities. These can be lucrative opportunities and can provide products for the web as well.

- TRACK YOUR PROGRESS
  Certain posts will get better responses than others. Learn from those. Was it you? Was it the content/subject matter? Was it the presentation? Knowing what works for you allows you to polish your work. That will help when approaching marketing partnerships.

HOW CAN YOU FIND A SPONSOR?

Quite simply, let brands know that you are open to collaborations. Along with the help of the platforms themselves willing to help top performers match with brands and marketers, numerous agencies will help you connect and match a brand with your influence. Many of Hollywood's top agencies now have influencer departments that are geared toward finding opportunities for top influencers with high follower numbers. But if you are willing to contact a brand directly, be professional and to the point. This is going to take time and energy. You will want to continue to work at an even pace so that brands can see you are reliable, promote new content heavily, and use hashtags when possible as brands notice them.

CREATE A PRESS KIT

- DO NOT SEND TO BRANDS UNSOLICITED
  Even if you contact the brand directly, let them know that you have a press kit available and they will ask for it, if they are interested.

- WHAT SHOULD IT INCLUDE?
  Ideally, it should consist of a maximum of five pages:

      COVER PAGE
      BRIEF BIO AND STORY OF BLOG/INFLUENCE
      PHOTO
      STATS AND DELIVERABLES—STATS TRACKER
      CONTACT INFO

PITCHING THE BRAND

Should a meeting happen with a brand, remember you only get one chance at a first impression. The more you know about their company, the more impressive you look to them. It shows investment on your part. Potentially, you are not the only person they are looking at...you will want to stand out. But again, your ability to stand out is exactly how you have become an influencer in the first place and the very reason you are in the room now.

- WHAT ARE YOU WORTH TO THEM?
  It is not what you think you are worth. It is all about what they think you are worth. Do your research to understand what they are looking for in an influencer, how they are spending their marketing dollars, knowing whom they consider their target audience (and plan to let them know how you can reach them), and learn how what you do can mesh with what they do. The more information you have, the better you can understand whether their offer of compensation is fair.

- SET A PAYMENT TERM
  Make sure you understand how and when you are getting paid.

WHAT ARE YOU WORTH?

Standard fees for followers are:

- $10 FOR EVERY 1000 FOLLOWERS

- 50-80,000 FOLLOWERS = $200 PER POST

TOP INFLUENCERS

Forbes and other money-tracking sources constantly update the latest top earners and top influencers. It is a moveable feast. Many, you should understand, have made their sizable paychecks not just from the web but have parlayed their influence into successful business ventures. Are you prepared to do that? This is a good way to start. It is always worth asking yourself two questions: "What is my end game?" & "What am I in this for?" Because it takes work to get to where these people have gotten. I encourage you to look up these people and others and decide for yourself, just what makes them so successful.

- JIMMY DONALDSON "MR. BEAST" --$54 MILLION—162 MIL FOLLOWERS

- JAKE PAUL--$45 MILLION—57 MIL FOLLOWERS

- CHARLI D'AMELIO--$17.5 MILION—203 MIL FOLLOWERS

- ALEXANDRA COOPER "CALL ME DADDY" --$20 MILLION—3.6 MIL FOLLOWERS

- ELLIOT TEBELE "FUCKJERRY" --$30 MILLION—20 MIL FOLLOWERS

- EMMA CHAMBERLAIN--$12 MILLION—27 MIL FOLLOWERS

- HUDA KATTAN--$13 MILLION—63 MIL FOLLOWERS

- RHETT & LINK-$30 MILLION—12 MILL FOLLOWERS

- KHABY LAME--$10 MILLION—231 MIL FOLLOWERS

- ADDISON RAE EASTERLING--$8.5 MILLION—133MIL FOLLOWERS

PUBLIC SPEAKING

PUBLIC SPEAKING

WHY ARE YOU TAKING CENTER STAGE?

By taking center stage, you could quite literally be stepping out on the center of a stage as a motivational speaker, a corporate spokesperson, or an instructor. But public speaking encompasses much more than that. From being interviewed for any number of reasons or events to becoming the face of a product or business, your ability to be personable, informative, direct, precise, knowledgeable, trusted, and more can make or break the message behind your presentation.

In today's world, social media—media in general—is an omnipresent and necessary tool for messaging. But it is a double edge sword. You need it to send the right message to the greatest possible audience and, yet an unwitting slip of the tongue or out-of-

context statement can misdirect the message completely. You need to know what the media needs and match it to your needs. Alternatively, effective live speaking from a podium or a stage relies on a different skillset—utilizing effective voice techniques, body language, and personality to speak with you and sometimes for you.

But the two aren't separate entities. Techniques you learn as an interviewee and those you develop for the stage or audience with benefit each other. As such, we will divide this part of the book into two sections: part one will deal with being interviewed and part two will take on you becoming a spokesperson.

PART ONE:

BEING INTERVIEWED

There are many reasons why you may find yourself in front of a microphone—some self-serving, some defensive, or unpleasant. You must be prepared for it all as it is your credibility at stake in all cases. Whether you have asked to do the interview, or the interviewer has solicited you, you must be prepared for whatever comes your way and be on top of your game. Don't jump at the chance to be in front of the camera. Think about it, debate the pros and cons, formulate the message, and given the time, practice. You are always better served by being prepared. The following three points should get you thinking:

WHAT FOR...

What is the purpose of the interview?

- Did you call for an interview? Are you being introduced as the new face or voice of the product or business, is there a message or mission statement that needs to be clarified or, worse, a mistake that needs to be rectified?

- Were you asked for an interview? Are you on the offensive or defensive?

To that end:

FIRST QUESTION: DO I WANT TO DO THIS INTERVIEW?

Is there anything to be gained by doing this interview? Is there positive publicity to be had? Similarly, will you look like you are hiding or evading by choosing not to appear? But in either case, do your homework with the interviewer:

- WHY ARE THEY WANTING OR DOING THIS INTERVIEW?
  What is in it for them? Is this just a general assignment beat
  or are they invested in a bigger more layered story that can
  serve you better?

- ANGLE OF THE STORY
  Are you the subject of the story or is your subject an example
  of a larger story? As such you may end up being just a line or
  two mentioned in an otherwise big piece. Will that serve your
  needs? Perhaps any exposure is good exposure. This is something you have to weigh out.

- FORMAT
  Asking the format of the segment clarifies whether it is a
  profile piece, a news piece, a lifestyles piece, etc.; and that will
  determine your position as favorable or not.

- LENGTH OF INTERVIEW
  How long will the interview take versus how long is the finished segment? Traditionally, a news package or segment
  is ninety seconds or a minute and a half. Therefore, is there
  a need to do a thirty-minute interview? Again, you have to
  weigh the benefits of what is on offer.

- OTHERS PARTICIPATING
  Are there other interviews on the same subject participating?

  ◊ Are you just one example of several?

  ◊ If it is a pro versus con segment, whichever side you are
    on, will you get a chance to rebut the opposition?

RESEARCH THE ORGANIZATION INTERVIEWING

Are they reputable news or information organization that will ad-
equately get your message across to the largest possible audience?

BE CAREFUL THAT THE REPORTER OR INTERVIEWER
HAS AN AGENDA

For your information, every interviewer has an agenda—whether it is passive or aggressive is arbitrary and according to the story. They are there to get a story and they start their questioning with a premise, therein lies the agenda. It is your agenda to have a clear message and work toward getting that message heard. Listen to the question carefully and make sure you can answer it by not getting off point.

For instance, if your message is that your company sells the best ice cream, and the question is: Why do you consider your ice cream to be the best? You can easily get your message across. But if the question is: Saying your ice cream is the best is simply subjective. Everyone has different tastes, different likes, and different tolerances even. How do you quantify saying a verbose claim like your ice cream is the best?

So, what do you do? Here are some options:

- You could take the stance of using the word "best" repeatedly. We have the "best" ingredients. We have done studies and chosen the flavors that people like "best."

- You could twist the answer to redefining the idea of "best." Is it the actual ice cream...or the experiences you are having when you are eating it?

- You could take all the negatives of the question and turn them into positives in your messaging. "We have embraced the diversity of different tastes, likes, and tolerances in creating a product that is liked for being different rather than the same old ice cream...we want a new experience, new flavors, and new tastes that will bring you a new option...one that is "best" for you.

SKIRTING AROUND "NO COMMENT"

You never want to have nothing to say or be forced to utter "no comment." You should always be prepared for the worst-case scenario. If you are asked a negative question, a "no comment" answer usually connotes you are trying to hide something, are less than honest or can't be trusted. A better way to answer is to skirt with a positive answer.

For example, if you were asked if you had an affair. How would you answer? And the first rule is: DON'T LIE. You will be found out every time.

- If the answer is yes, you did have that affair; you could answer by saying: "The privacy of my family is what is important here. They are aware of what your allegations are and we are dealing with them as a family unit in privacy."

- If the answer is no, you did not have the affair; but people don't believe your denial, you could answer by saying: "I am aware that these allegations exist and while I firmly deny the affair, you just have to look to the support of my family and friends as a second layer of verification of the truth. This is a private matter that only requires the support and understanding of those involved."

- If you are a public person and the denial does require public support, rethink that last line to say something more like: "I believe the public will support me the way my family and friends who know the truth already do."

That may have been an extreme example. But the point is the same regarding "no comment." Have a positive spin answer ready rather than saying nothing. Saying nothing means everyone else will speak for you.

OFF THE RECORD

There is always the opportunity to stipulate that certain topics or issues are off the table to talk about during an interview. But be cau-
tious, if they are important issues as to why the interviewer wanted
to talk to you in the first place, they may find clever ways to get you to
speak close to or around the subject matter and either make you look
uncomfortable, evasive or have something to hide.

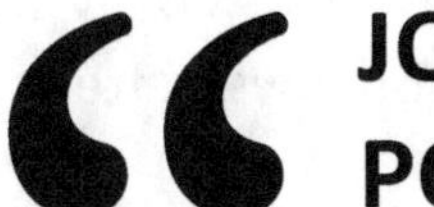

JOHN WILLIAMS STORY... POP GO THE POPS

In my early career, I had the honor of working with
the iconic British journalist Angela Rippon who had taken a sojourn
assignment for a year in Boston at the CBS affiliate as the Arts & Entertainment Correspondent. The arts were a big assignment in the
Boston area and there was so shortage of stories for us to choose to
cover.

During our tenure, one big story was the heated departure and then
comeback of legendary composer John Williams as conductor of the
Boston Symphony Orchestra. It had been many contentious months
between leaving and coming back and when Angela secured the
interview upon his return, it was stipulated that he would not talk
about the reasons for his leaving the Symphony in the first place.
Agreed.

During the interview, pleasantries were established and as agreed,
Angela did not ask about his leaving. Rather, she asked why he'd
come back. Inevitably, in answering that question he was forced
to elaborate on how things had changed for him to come back and
thereby insinuating what was wrong that drove
him out in the first place. Brilliant. Proving what is
sometimes off the record is not always off the plate.

DANGEROUS REPORTERS

Nefarious is maybe a better word to describe these types of reporters but they can be dangerous if you don't know how to handle them. And you have met them all before:

THE FRIENDLY GUY AT SOCIAL OCCASIONS

This type makes you feel like he is your best friend, "you can trust me", and "has your best interests at heart." The truth is, once he has your confidence, he believes you will tell your darkest secrets. DON'T. There is no reason that you can't entrust a journalist you have vetted. But as you are aware, not everyone is trustworthy.

THE QUIET GUY—MAKES YOU FEEL AWKWARD

There is something about the unnaturally shy personality that gets you to reach out and fill in the awkward silence. Again, this ploy of "aw shucks" etc. is just to get you to answer questions you think he needs to know but hasn't asked. Inevitably you will say too much.

THE JERK—AGGRESSIVE OR HOSTILE

Whether it is by a loud voice, body language, or repeating questions until he wears you down, this reporter's tactic is to browbeat you into submission. You may even think you are frustrated enough by this tactic to strike back and take control of the answers—in other words, give them. That is just what he wants—you to think that by answering his questions, you are in control. All you are is...answering questions you probably shouldn't be.

The following is a perfect example of how you can be tripped up without even knowing it.

" KITTY KELLY AND THAT DAMN DRESS

I was laying on a jetty that was jutting out into the Mediterranean Sea just off the beach in Cap d'Antibes in the South of France with two friends—one of whom being the renowned designer, Lindka Cierach, who is best known for designing the wedding gown for Sarah, Duchess of York. I was tearing through a delicious copy of Kitty Kelly's THE ROYALS which had been banned in Britain (officially "not printed" to avoid Britain's strict libel laws).

"Oh, that woman," Lindka huffed, pointing at my book.

"What's wrong with Kitty Kelly?" I asked. "I see you made the book in several places. Quotes and all."

"I have never given that woman an interview!" she snapped. "I never speak about my clients. Especially not to journalists and of all people, never about the Royals."

"Let's look you up," I pressed. "I know Kelly is meticulous with her bibliography notations." With that, I found Lindka's name in the back and it gave several page number references and notes as to where the conversations took place—one, in particular, was a Thanksgiving day dinner.
The following was more like strafing rather than simple conversation:

"Did you attend a Thanksgiving dinner party that she was at?" I prodded.

"Yes…" she muttered. And right then I knew she was done for. This is the way these things work. Informal conversations turn into recorded soundbites. That is the way some journalist such as Kitty

Kelly work. She knew she had a live one in Lindka.

"Do you remember speaking with her? Because she is a journalist.
If you spoke to her and didn't mention it was off the record. It was
fair game."

"Yes, I was there at Thanksgiving...but I didn't give an interview. I
would never speak about Sarah publicly..." Just then her cell phone
rang and she mouthed that it was coincidentally Sarah, Duchess
of York, calling in. She took the call. It seemed rather heated and
within earshot—not the kind of conversation you would have between a client and vendor. Certainly not one as important as the
Duchess. I turned to my other friend and we smiled. Lindka did not
attempt to be discreet.

Once finished and without provocation, she began, "That woman!
She is ordering several dresses...all the same...but she is picking fab-
rics that are unflattering to her figure. She won't listen to me at all.
I don't know how long I can go on working with her..."

She went on in great detail about the Duchess and her problems
she seemed to be having with her as a client. I was reveling in the
conversation as she had no idea of the hole in which she was digging
herself into.

"I thought you didn't talk about you clients...certainly not the Royals...in front of journalists," I shot back at her.

"I don't!" she shot back indignantly.

"Who do you think I am? This is a great story I can run with. Wit-
nessed even by a third party."

She looked panicked and confused, not quite sure what she had done. "This is how Kitty Kelly does her work. You speak and she listens," I pointed out. She continued to plead her case of innocence, and I suggested that her conversations should be called "cocktale" conversations instead of cocktail conversations.

SECOND QUESTION: IS THERE A CRISIS?

A crisis is defined as an event or incident precipitated by an accidental occurrence that garners mass media attention for an ongoing and indeterminate amount of time. It can be a product, business, or individual-based situation, but the issues are always the same:

    a. THERE IS GOING TO BE PAIN/HURT TO THE PRODUCT
No matter what the situation, the product you are selling is going to suffer a blow. You are going to have to get in front of the situation immediately. What is the plan? Formulate and deliver. But be prepared to formulate a message of repair and recovery for the product or there is no coming back.

    b. THERE IS ALWAYS A GOOD GUY AND A BAD GUY
Which role do you play?

- The bad guy caused the problem and has to take responsibility

- The good guy is there to fix the problem

    c. COMMUNICATE IMMEDIATELY
Getting in front of the narrative immediately is important. Ignoring the situation or delaying action is only going to

make things worse. Coming forward with a positive, pro-active message and game plan shows action to get things done, that you are in charge and you will be able to better control the narrative.

d. THERE IS ALWAYS A VICTIM AND THE MEDIA
SIDES WITH THE VICTIMS
Remember to be empathic to those affected by the crisis. You don't want to be a bully, disrespectful or disengaged. People will not trust that you are there to help or ready to resolve the situation

e. THE SPOKESPERSON MUST BE WELL CHOSEN
Who is the best voice or face of the situation?

- Is it a corporate head? Perhaps if the situation is a larger issue within a big, structured problem. Go to the top for clarity and to show "the buck stops" at the top.

- Is it a blue-collar person? If this is a worker or "every person" situation, perhaps someone the victims can relate to is more appropriate.

- If it is a personal issue, put the person front and center. Do not hide them behind a spokesperson "on their behalf." It shows insincerity at the very least and something to hide or guilt at the worst.

f. SOCIAL MEDIA IS A FACTOR
Things can escalate quickly over social media. Do not ignore addressing these platforms and options to get your message out.

g. BE HONEST TRUTHFUL AND UPFRONT
While you must protect the integrity of your asset, you must be honest about what this crisis is all about. You

can be judicious about the information you give out, but always make sure it is truthful. A lie or misrepresentation can cripple your side of the argument.

h.   APOLOGIZE RIGHT AWAY
If you are responsible, you are responsible. Own up and apologize to move forward. If there is a question of responsibility, offer to apologize that the situation occurred but do not incriminate yourself.

i.   LAWYERS CAN MAKE IT WORSE
A team of lawyers or lawyers as spokespeople can make you appear as you need them. They connote guilt and that something illegal occurred. Find a more appropriate "spokes-figure" to represent the messaging, even if there is a law team behind it.

j.   STAY COOL
Never let them see you sweat. This may be a tense time, but you have to look like you are confident and in control. If not, you radiate that there is a problem and you are hiding something.

k.   BE PREPARED FOR THE AMBUSH INTERVIEW
Simply put, the ambush interview is being attacked by questions that come out of the left field. The classic example is: "Do you beat your wife?" The obvious answer is "No." The follow-up question then becomes "So do you deny that you beat your wife?" The story becomes that you deny beating your wife, not that you don't beat your wife at all. While you can't know an ambush is coming, you can prepare for the situation:

- PLEDGE TO LEARN MORE
  This pertains to questions that allude to you not

being knowledgeable about the issue. You can say something to the effect of: "While I understand there may have been some confusion over previous comments, we, as an institution are committed to educating ourselves on all aspects of the situation, pro, and con, and will comment accordingly."

- TALK ABOUT WHAT YOU DO KNOW
  You don't want to be caught talking about information you can't verify or fully understand and be proven wrong. So don't talk about what you don't know, deflect to talking points you can control. Again, you could answer by saying something akin to: "While I understand there may have been some confusion over previous comments, what I do know is this...."

- GENERALIZE
  It is better to say something over nothing. You can always list generalizations but only if they are on point and don't make you look like you are babbling. Again, less is more when you are not being specific. You can answer with something which begins with: "That is an interesting point, but what we have come to understand is this..."

WHEN THE GOING GOT TOUGH... EVERYONE WENT TO HOWARD BRAGMAN

I had known the PR guru Howard Bragman and worked with his agencies for the better part of three decades. I first came to know of Bragman, Nyman, Caferelli—the boutique powerhouse agency that represented the likes of Kate Hudson, Cameron Diaz, Whoopie Goldberg, and Barry Manilow—as an entertainment reporter. Over the years, BNC merged and morphed as did Bragman who before his recent untimely death was considered THE man to see when it came to crisis management with his LA BREA MEDIA. As a well-known media consultant for news outlets, he was the go-to 'spokes mouth' when anyone who is anyone steps off point. Why was he so good at correcting the bad? Because public relations was all about controlling the media, controlling the message. There is no difference in creating a brand on the positive side than there is in putting out a fire on the negative side. Upon hearing of his passing, I couldn't help but visit his website where he generously offers nuggets of information for you to digest such as his ten commandments of PR (excerpted from his book "WHERE'S MY FIFTEEN MINUTES":

—ALL PRESS IS NOT GOOD PRESS: Do what you can to keep your private life private. Social media is a killer. If you want to be naughty, keep it behind closed doors. Try to create a public persona that radiates good.

—PERCEPTION IS REALITY: Don't be fooled into thinking that the truth would get in the way of a good story.

—CREATE A BRAND: You are not your career; you are your brand. The idea is to make that brand multi-faceted and well-respected. It is no good to just be good at one thing anymore.

—THE TRUTH SEEKS ITS OWN LEVEL: Thanks to the internet, there are no secrets anymore. If you have something to hide, it will eventually surface.

—ENERGIZE A BASE: Figure out who your followers are and work with them.

—THE MEDIA WILL NOT WAIT FOR YOU: You should always play offense, not defense. If you do not have a message or have nothing to say…you should not be doing an interview.

—THERE IS NO WALL BETWEEN PUBLIC AND PRIVATE: Work your public self.

—THE MEDIUM IS STILL THE MESSAGE: More media means more landmines. Stick to media that works for your message.

And when it comes to a PR Crisis, Bragman was a specialist. He handled everything and everyone from corporations to celebrities and politicians who may have found themselves…shall we say compromised. His advice was straight forward and direct. You can't hide from the truth.

In his book, he defined it best:

A PR crisis occurs when a person or company receives overwhelmingly negative publicity from the media and the general public. These crises can do serious damage, resulting in loss of income, unemployment, and public humiliation. With social media so readily accessible all around the world, it's never been a worse time to slip up in the public eye. News travels fast. The truth doesn't matter. Once a crisis gets online and goes viral, there's very little you can do to stop the juggernaut of information.

It's important to be able to differentiate between an embarrassing mistake and a public relations crisis. We all make mistakes, and with the amount of content being generated to stay relevant, mistakes are more likely than ever to happen. Not every mistake is a crisis.

To determine if you have a PR crisis on your hands, ask yourself the following questions:

—Will this upset stakeholders and potentially damage the workflow productivity of my company?
—Was anyone killed or injured?
—Will we lose money? Is our bottom line at risk?
—Will this do damage our brand and reputation? Will we lose followers, stakeholders, --customers, or investors?

If you answer "yes" to just one of these questions, you might be in trouble, but you're not in a crisis situation. Most likely, you're dealing with a negative review or embarrassing social post. However, if you answer "yes" to two of these questions, then you need to be on high alert and ready to act. If you answered yes to three or maybe even four of these questions, well, buckle up. You're in full crisis PR mode. Do. Not. Panic. The worst thing you can do is overreact. The second worst thing you can do is under-react. Your response needs to be quick, measured, and thoughtful. It's important that you pay attention to what is being said online about your company to assess how much damage has been done. This is called Social Listening. If the comments online have taken a sharp shift towards a negative trend, your PR crisis is likely well on its way to worsening. If you haven't already pre-planned your crisis management, don't wait a moment longer.

- The following are real-life examples that Freden experienced whereby the subject matter of the crisis was simply unprepared and the result was a failure to communicate:

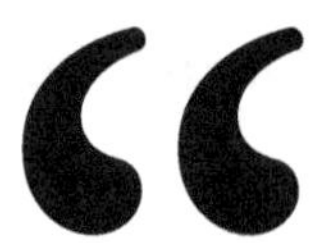# ELIZABETH TAYLOR...A HEADACHE

When Elizabeth Taylor was diagnosed with what was perceived to be a life-threatening brain tumor, I did my homework. I went to interview the head of neurological oncology at a prestigious Los Angeles cancer institute to get clarification on her condition. The doctor explained her situation and when the interview ended he went "off the record" to say that he would never have operated. "Why?" I asked. He stated bluntly that he wouldn't want to be the doctor known to have killed Elizabeth Taylor on the operating table. I questioned whether her life was in that much danger. And again, he said yes. Moreover, when you do any surgery on the brain, you leave behind scar tissue that the body sees as a foreign body and may attack it, leaving the patient vulnerable to stroke-like symptoms and a lifetime of seizures. That was information I assumed every reporter was gathering at the time.

When the press conference was held, announcing Ms. Taylor had come through the surgery, a brief statement was made highlighting that she was aware and had spoken and then the surgical team opened the floor up for questions. Most of them were innocuous such as: how long she would be in the hospital or what were her first words. I rose my hand and asked: "Given that there is now scar tissue in her brain, is there any concern about the obvious threat of seizures or stroke-like symptoms plaguing her over her lifetime?" Rather than answering the question at all, the press conference was shut down and the doctors were escorted away immediately.

What did they do wrong? They left the world's media believing that the only answer to my supposition question was an affirmative as they never gave us a reason to dispel the threat. You can imagine how the story ran that evening.

What they should have done was to deflect: "While we understand

the risks involved with any invasive brain surgery, the percentages
of such risks resulting in the symptoms you have stated are XXXX
and we believe due to the nature of Ms. Taylor's condition we think
those risks are further mitigated by..."

A STAR...NOT OUT, WHAT'S IT ABOUT

A rather A-List star in Hollywood is constantly deflecting rumors that
he has had gay relationships. Anyone who hints he might be gay
gets slapped with a lawsuit amounting to tens of millions of dollars.
In this case, he lets his lawyers do the talking for him. I have suggested that he face the accusations with plausible deniability and issue
a statement that amounts to the following: I am an actor. It is my
job to attract fans. If they are gay and believe me to be gay to relate
to me, that is fine with me. I am doing my job. I have gay friends.
If you see me embracing a man, it is because I love my friends and
don't find shame in expressing that love. Does that mean I am gay?
I will remind you that I have been married to two beautiful women
and have beautiful children whom I hope one day will be as lucky as
I am to have as diverse a group of loving friends as I have.

The value of that statement is that no one can accuse him of anything more than friendship. It addresses the issue without blame
or accusations. Instead, the actor appears to be hiding from the
rumors and has something to hide from. It is not a good look not to
be in front of the message.

THE FUR FLIES

While I was working on GMTV for Great Britain, I primarily covered
Hollywood within the entertainment, lifestyles, and pop-culture
genres. One story which was assigned to me via London was the

then phenomenon of the resurgence of real fur in haute couture. My assignment was to find an expert who could talk about the popularity of fur in fashion. Dutifully, I secured the manager of one of Beverly Hills' top furriers. He agreed to the interview, which would be live to London from our Los Angeles studio, on the condition that it would not be a debate between him and an anti-fur protestor. I assured him that was not the thrust of the story...or so I was led to believe. The anchorwoman in London, a staunch anti-fur activist, had a different agenda.

The question was asked as to why he felt fur was making a comeback. He answered succinctly that the luxury and feel of fur were highly desirable. But before he could quite finish his thought, the anchorwoman ambushed him with: "I am sure that the animals that were slaughtered felt their fur was both a luxury and they desired to keep it on their backs." The furrier froze. So she continued. "You can't even comment because you know I am right? This is a bloody and cruel and unnecessary business for which you have blood on your hands."

He was so taken aback; he couldn't speak and she continued to berate him to the other anchors on the sofa back in London. "Look at him. He has nothing to say. Because he knows I am right..." He didn't answer because he was holding back the urge to cry.

While I was inevitably blamed by the furrier for the disaster and the anchorwoman, who had crossed all journalist lines of neutrality wasn't even reprimanded, the furrier could have responded thusly: There are always faux fur alternatives if you disagree with the industry. It is a personal choice. Your choice is not in keeping with what designers feel today's marketplace is looking for.

At that point, I simply would have gotten up and left. There is no

time for an interview to devolve into a radical attack. State your position and leave it alone. As Michelle Obama famously stated: "If they go low, we go high." There is something to that.

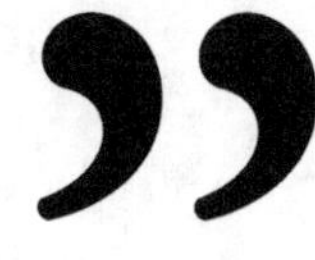

THIRD QUESTION: IS THIS ALL ABOUT PRO-MOTION?

Promotion, more than ever, requires a strong presence and personality which should match the messaging. Promotions generally fall into three basic departments:

- ◊ SELF—Are you promoting yourself as an expert, your talent, or a skillset?

- ◊ PRODUCT—Are you the spokesperson for a particular product or brand?

- ◊ BUSINESS—Do you represent the interests of a business or corporate structure?

But no matter what the category, the canons of messaging and delivery remain the same:

1 WHAT IS YOUR MESSAGE?
   Before you start speaking, think about the nature of what you need to say. Does the message need to take into account any of the following considerations?

   - ◊ Is the message fact of results based?

   - ◊ Is the message about problem-solving or solution based?

◊ Is it a call to action?

◊ Does it outline benefits, providing selling points to clients or buyers?

2. CRAFTING THE DELIVERY

Delivering an effective message is a matter of two points:

◊ WHAT YOU WANT TO SAY

> ◊ Make sure your message is clear and easy to understand. Do not confuse the audience. Be on point and direct. Repeating the message is a good thing. An overuse of examples to drive a point…may drive the audience away.
>
> ◊ If you are being interviewed, remember to re-peat the message in the answer. Don't assume the question will appear in the finished seg-ment. So, you want to make sure the message is not lost to editing.
>
> ◊ Be careful about giving personal opinions. It should be about the facts, not your interpreta-tion of the facts.

◊ WHAT THE AUDIENCE NEEDS TO HEAR

> ◊ STORIES
> The use of anecdotes and stories as examples gives the audience something to relate to. Let the audience go on the ride with you. The fol-lowing are some examples of plot structures in which you can envelop your messaging:
>
> > i. THE CHALLENGE: David versus Goliath, Rags to Riches.

   ii. THE CONNECTION: People who develop a relationship that bridges a gap.

   iii. THE CREATIVITY: Breakthroughs, Puzzle Solving, Innovative Problem Solving.

◊ STATS

If you are going to use statistics to emphasize a point, remember the following:

   i. Make the example personal to the audience.

   ii. Use ratios.

   iii. Be specific rather than using percentages. Such as saying 3 out of every 4 women are dark-haired. Rather than saying 3/4's of woman dye their hair.

◊ CREATING THE SOUNDBITE

When answering a reporter, make sure the message is complete should though, and try to sound natural as if you just made it up on the fly. It is that much better when people believe something profound is impromptu.

An example of a resonating impromptu statement is when Rodney King was beaten by the police in an incident that sparked the infamous L.A. riots. King, when interviewed about it, uttered: "CAN'T WE ALL JUST GET ALONG." It became an anthem for peace for decades.

The following are devices that grab the audience:

   i. USE METAPHORS & ANALOGIES

   ii. THE LAW OF THREES: Tell them your mes-

sage, repeat the message and then tell
them what they just heard.

iii. AVOID RHETORICAL QUESTIONS

iv. USE CONTRASTS OR PARADOXES

v. THERE IS POWER IN BEING DEFINITIVE

vi. USE SUPERLATIVES

vii. USE POP CULTURE REFERENCES AS EXAM-
PLES

viii. EMOTION—Feel the pain and/or pleasure
with the audience.

ix. SURPRISE TWIST—During a debate, when
Florida Republican Governor DeSantis
was asked by his Gubernatorial opponent
Charlie Crist if DeSantis was going to run for
President against the much older President
Biden in 2022, he responded that the only
old donkey he was looking to knock off was
Crist.

x. TWEAKED CLICHES—Puns, clichés, alliteration...the audience will react to them.

PRESENTATION

CONTROLLING YOURSELF

BODY LANGUAGE

a. AVOID CLOSED BODY LANGUAGE
You don't want to be hunched over, arms crossed, or even have your hands clasped. All of that says you are closed from your audience. You want to be open to them and they, in turn, will feel more like you are being open with them.

b. AVOID BIG GESTURES
Big arm gestures or loud laughter for instance can be distracting and suddenly the audience is watching you and not listening to you.

c. GOOD POSTURE
Sit up. It is as simple as that. You want to look like you are not slouched or slovenly.

d. THEY WON'T HEAR YOU IF YOU ARE DISTRACT-ING
You don't want to do anything distracting. You may want to accentuate or punctuate but if you become too overt, again, you are distracting the audience. They are no longer listening; they will feel you are performing.

VOICE

- VOLUME AND PACE
You should speak at a consistent volume, not suddenly high or low unless for effect, and with a steady pace that the audience can follow. You don't want to seem rushed or out of breath.

- **AVOID SILENCES…UNLESS WELL-TIME PAUSES**
  It is one thing to pause for dramatic effect. It is another thing altogether to simply stop speaking. People will believe that you have lost your way and that you are not as knowledgeable as you are trying to present.

- **DEEP BREATHS**
  Control your breathing. Practice diaphragmatically breathing rather than panting. It is like singing.

- **AVOID AHHHS AND UHHHS**
  Annoying ahs, uhs, or words frequently used such as "Like", will only annoy and distract the audience. Practice your speaking to avoid falling into the trap.

ENERGY

Keep your energy high. This is important. Your energy level is infectious. If you are upbeat and energetic, the audience is with you and paying attention. Low energy begets low energy and can cause the audience to be inattentive and easily distracted.

EYE CONTACT

If you can make eye contact, do. People want to know that you are connecting with them and that they are being understood and listened to as well as being talked to.   In a live audience, setting try to make eye contact with as many people as you can, for as many people as possible to feel they have made a connection. In a television experience, look directly at the interviewer. A wandering eye will make the audience feel like you don't care about your message.

WHAT TO WEAR
(The following was discussed in the TELEVISION segment but it is worth reiterating. So, we have repeated the information to keep mindful.)

BE TRUE TO YOUR BRAND
There is an old expression: clothes make the man. I will go further and say that clothes make the brand—and you are the brand you are trying to sell. Packaging any product is an integral part of marketing. Think of your look as packaging. You want the packaging to comple-ment, help deliver the message subliminally and literally, and define a consistency of presence. Ask yourself:

- *Are you formal?*

- *Are you informal?*

    Does that mean prep school chic, sporty, or haute couture?

When you can define your brand and match it with a look remember there is always room for some cross-pollinating. To be effective in changing up your look for your brand, rely on being consistent with making sure the look matches the message:

◊ *FOR MEN:*
    A suit and tie say authority but so can solid colors if a suit and tie are not right for a particular setting. But feel free to pick non-traditional suits such as windowpane fabrics rather than a simple blue suit if you wish to evoke a younger point of view. But, having to defer to a staid and formal message or brand is no excuse not to have a well-tailored, stylized suit along with which you can make a bold statement with a colorful or pat-terned tie.

*Why can jeans and a black turtleneck be so effective a look?
Neutrality. Pair that with a black sports jacket and you've
amped up the package. You could make the statement bolder
with loafer shoes and no socks. All together you exude casual
chic confidence.*

*There is no distraction from the message and the delivery.
You can say anything with credibility if you choose a neutral
palette. If that look seemed familiar. It was the uniform of the
late Steve Jobs, the head of Apple, who didn't do too badly for
himself.*

◊   *FOR WOMEN:*
*Women have far more choices facing them. I believe con-
sistency is the key. Pick a look, a style, a designer, a fabric,
color palette that works and stick with it. Hillary Clinton, for
instance, stays with pant suits and no handbags. I would
recommend staying away from loud patterns UNLESS that is a
gimmick or statement you are trying to make specifically. And
defer to classic dressing rather than trends. Simple is sometimes smarter and less distracting than giving the audience
something to critique.*

*LOOK LIKE WHAT YOU ARE TRYING TO SAY—BE YOURSELF
Above all else, you must be comfortable. You must never feel
as if you are putting on a costume. You will inevitably turn
your presentation into a performance.
KNOW HOW TO DO YOUR MAKEUP*

*As we discussed, no two lighting or setting situations will be
the same. You must know how to do the basics of make-up
application to not appear washed out or sickly under harsh
lighting. THIS APPLIES TO MEN AS WELL.*

THE SETTING

Where you speak from can be as important as the message itself. It too is sending a message. The more formal the setting, the more serious the messaging, and vice versa. The following a just a few examples of traditional location settings and what they may be saying to your audience:

◊ BEHIND THE DESK:
This is usually meant for more formal, declarative messages. This is very no-nonsense, straight-to-the-point information.

◊ SITTING AT THE EDGE OF THE DESK
This location indicates that the message has facts that are important to you but are to be delivered in a much more conversational manner. Giving the boss, for instance, a more "of the worker" sensibility.

◊ AT A PODIUM
Many times, this setting is used for announcements and followed by a question-and-answer session.

◊ ON LOCATION
This is a much more informal option: sitting by a fireplace, walking on a beach, having a coffee at a café all say "you can relax. I have something you need to hear...but there is nothing to worry about..." OR mitigates the crisis.

◊ ZOOM OR SKYPE
If you are using this medium regularly, you may want to think about the following:

- Set up a regular location where the background is neutral and not distracting.

- Set the computer camera on a slightly higher angle and

invest in a ring light for a flattering look.

- Limit your movements while on camera as the digital connection isn't always consistent and may be jittery or on a time delay which is exacerbated with movement.

- Look into the camera and not at the screen when speaking. The camera will direct your eye line to the interviewer or audience and not have you appear to be looking off in the distance. It may seem awkward to do but the result will be far more effective.

AUDIENCE FOCUSED

While you should look the reporter in the eye to keep focus, remember the reporter is not your audience, the viewer is. That begs these points:

◊ HOW BIG IS THE AUDIENCE?
Are you addressing several people or a large crowd? Whom are you trying to reach? If you are trying to rally a crowd you may want to be more bombastic; a small crowd may require you to be demurer.

◊ WHAT IS THEIR LEVEL OF KNOWLEDGE?
Are you trying to explain or educate the audience? As such, make sure your facts are clear, concise, and easily understandable in stand-alone sound bites. Do not be choppy or haphazard with information or the segment will also be choppy and haphazard, and the message may be lost.

◊ CALLING REPORTERS BY NAME CHANGES FOCUS
Calling a reporter by his/her name takes the focus from the viewer. Remember whom you are trying to reach. The reporter is not your audience. Eye contact is enough. The reporter knows you are talking to him/her.

◊ DEFINE TECHNICAL INFO
If anything is very technical in your dialogue, you can assume
the audience may not be clear on its meaning or significance.
Take a moment to clarify what you are talking about so the
messaging is not lost in the minutia.

HOW DO YOU CONTROL THE NARRATIVE?

It is your job to take advantage of the opportunity of being interviewed. Do not be a passive participant. Make sure you drive the
answers to the questions to your message rather than let the questions take you in a direction off-point.

◊ DON'T EDUCATE THE REPORTER...THEY SHOULD KNOW
THE FACTS
You are there to speak to the audience. The reporter
should be aware of why you are there to speak and why
they chose to speak to you. If they ask simplistic questions, direct the answers to your message. Should the
questions be off-point, answer the question briefly and
then bring the answer back relatedly to your message.
Do not let the reporter lead you astray. You have a short
amount of time to get, maybe only one or two questions—make them count; maximize the content.

PART TWO:

BECOMING A SPOKESPERSON

Who are you and what are you going to represent?

CORPORATE

As we have indicated, more and more, corporate entities require spokespeople to face the camera to be the voice of the management message—from Walmart to Wall Street. Be it the CEO, public relations representative, or ta notable 'face' of the brand, the spokesperson must be dynamic, assertive, clear, likable, and trustworthy. Gone are the days when a simple press release will suffice. The media wants to put a face and a voice to the issues, both pros, and cons. You should never unwittingly find yourself in front of the camera. You should know that you will be there and be prepared. Incorporate the lessons learned from part one of this section to hone your skills but remember the following points:

1. WHAT IS YOUR EXPERTISE?
    On what subject or area of your corporation are you able to speak successfully and intelligently? If you can't speak with authority on an area of expertise...DON'T! There is nothing wrong with incorporating multiple spokespeople for multiple areas of expertise. For instance:

    - LEGAL

    - BUSINESS

    - MEDICAL

2. WHAT WILL BE THE NEED TO SPEAK PUBLICALLY?
    Make sure you are always aware of your mission. You want to
    always be on point.

    - PUBLIC RELATIONS

    - Are you trying to clarify your company's position on a
      particular issue?

    - CORPORATE INFORMATION

    - Explaining how a product or process works.

    - CRISIS MANAGEMENT

    - (Refer to the aforementioned segment)

3. IN ALL CASES, ESTABLISH:

    ◊ CREDIBILITY
       Yes, your credentials matter...but so do vocal tone, body
       language, and expertise. All will play a difference in add-
       ing or subtracting to establish your credibility. I will break
       down how you present yourself as to your credibility.

    ◊ TRUST
       Similarly, I will break down what you say and how you
       say it as your trustworthiness. Can your audience believe
       what you are saying? Do not plead in what you are saying.
       But there is a factor of winning the audience over with a
       convincing argument. If you can keep on point without
       shedding doubt, you inevitably earn trust.

    ◊ AUTHORITY
       Are you an authority, an expert? You need to estab-
       lish your knowledge of the subject matter, situation, or
       product from the onset. If your audience questions your

knowledge, they will question you as an authority, begin not to trust you and you will lose credibility.

◊ LEADERSHIP
Even if you don't hold a leadership position within the corporate structure of the company, you have to take a leadership role in front of the camera. If the audience feels that you are a 'nobody' within the corporate structure, they are not going to pay attention to the company message.

◊ CLEAR UNDERSTANDING

i. IN MESSAGING

1. WHAT IS THE POINT?
Make sure there is a clear, consistent, concise message that can translate to multiple media platforms.

2. WHAT IS THE END GAME?
Are you trying to reach a mass audience or a select group with a new corporate image or a limited specific message? What you are trying to say and how you deliver the message will depend on those kinds of factors and you will have to be able to pivot according to those parameters.

ii. WHOM YOU ARE SPEAKING TO: THE MEDIA, SHAREHOLDERS, INTERNAL MOTIVATIONAL COACH, etc.
Does the message change with the makeup of the audience? If so, make sure you are on point with the audience you are trying to reach.

iii. HAVE ANSWERS TO EXPECTED QUESTIONS
Should you open up your presentation to a question & answer segment, be prepared with your answers. It will behoove you to refer back to how to prepare.
(Refer back to the interviewing segment/ Crisis Management in Part One of this section of the book.)

◊ DON'T USE "NO COMMENT"

◊ TRANSPARENCY—NOTHING EVASIVE
Honesty, honesty, honesty. You don't have to give away the corporate vault of secrets. But be honest and upfront when dealing with an audience of the media.

SPEAKING ENGAGEMENTS

You may find yourself both asked to speak as a lucrative career option in self-promotion or a product promotion or required to speak for your job. In any case, speaking to an audience, large or intimate, is an art form. Those willing to handle the craft will find themselves becoming creative producers—thinking about everything from content development, writing, staging, and performing. Others will see this as a gratifying opportunity to empower an audience.

Some people are natural performers while others have stage fright. Again, in either case, the job must be done and there are basic tools you can use to polish the process (in the case of the "performer") or ease the hesitancy (in the case of the "frightened").

BODY LANGUAGE

We have talked about the importance of body language before in this book. But it is so important when it comes to live speaking engagements. You are guiding the audience through the experience and you need to be aware at all times of not only what you are saying but how you are delivering the information or message. It can be highly effective with body language enhancement...or lost with a bland, monotone delivery. Effective body language breaks down into three categories:

a. THOUGHTS: SOMETHING WE KNOW
We present this through techniques that emphasize the cognitive thinking process like taking a pregnant pause in your delivery or being contemplative.

b. EMOTION: SOMETHING WE FEEL
Emoting brings the audience along with what they are supposed to feel. Can you make them laugh or bring them to tears?

c. ACTION: SOMETHING WE DO
This is the simple use of gestures just to emphasize a point or make a point, such as smiling, using a range of expressions, and having an open posture.

First, do a cold read. Familiarize yourself with your material. And then practice your speech in the mirror. Why? See what the audience sees. Coordinate the previous technique suggestions where applicable. You will see a difference.

CONNECTING IS KEY

This is crucial for establishing the perception of leadership—that you are the expert in the topic for which you are talking and that you are worth the audience's investment in listening.

NOT JUST HOW...BUT WHY DO YOU WANT TO CONNECT
Think about the reason you are there and why the audience is there. Are you the "teacher" and they the "students"? Are you selling something, and they are the buyers? Are you the philosopher, commentator, or editorialist and are they the listener? There are many incarnations to this equation...but the bottom line is: there must be a relationship between the speaker, content, and audience. Here are some basic points to establish or think about connectivity:

FIND COMMON GROUND

- WHO IS YOUR AUDIENCE
  I am not talking about knowing the number of people or that you are in an auditorium in Memphis. I want you to know that they are gay, religious leaders, senior citizens, young adults, or of a specific ethnic background. This may significantly change your approach to connectivity and even content. The worst assumption you can make is that you already know what the audience wants or is there to hear and you become indifferent to the subtleties and nuances of what they need from you.

- SHARE EXCITEMENT ABOUT BEING WITH THEM
  Make sure they know you want to be there as much as they want to be there with you.

- IT'S NOT ABOUT ME
  It is all about the audience. You are delivering a service to them...as far as they are concerned...so deliver it. That

isn't to say you are not the star of the show and they are
not excited to see you. Feel free to play off that but with
a certain amount of humility and self-deprecation. Thank
them for their interest.

- ESTABLISH TRUST
  The audience must trust you to buy into what you are saying. These points will help you establish that trust:

- SHARE STORIES, ILLUSTRATIONS, ANECDOTES
  Personal examples always provide a "been there with
  you" sensibility.

- BE A FRIEND
  Establish a closeness. "We are in this together...OR...I am
  here for you."

- YOU CAN BE VULNERABLE
  You are human too. Showing vulnerability such as "I have
  made that same mistake..." turns you into a person and
  not just a robotic spokesperson.

- PEOPLE WHO FAIL TO BELIEVE THEY ARE MORE IMPOR-
  TANT THAN THE AUDIENCE

- BE SIMPLE BUT EFFECTIVE—LET THEM KNOW YOU ARE
  THERE TO ADD VALUE
  People's time and actual money (if they have had to pay to
  hear you speak) is an investment. Make that investment
  turn into a dividend. They need to know that what you
  have to say is going to add value to their lives. Remind
  them in points why what you are saying is value added.
  But NEVER say things like: "This is why you spent $100
  to be here"...OR..."If you buy my book you will be better
  off..." Try an approach more along the lines of: "An adjust-
  ment in thought may take you in a more positive direction
  such as..." Be fluid and navigate with the audience and
  not against the tide.

- **BE INTERESTING**
  The audience is expecting to receive a performance, information, advice...you name it. They are not there to give. As the saying goes: there are no bad audiences, just bad speakers. One way to gain their interest is to encourage interaction: ask questions to individuals or the group and react accordingly. Make them part of the presentation.

- **BE INSPIRING/MEMORABLE**
  In so doing, your message will stick.

- **BE AUTHENTIC**
  This goes to credibility. If you prove your authenticity, you have achieved your credibility and trustworthiness. The following are points that you can include in your presentation to magnify your authenticity.

INSIGHT—WHAT DO YOU KNOW
SUCCESS---WHAT HAVE YOU DONE
ABILITY—WHAT CAN YOU DO
SACRIFICE—HOW HAVE YOU LIVED

IT REQUIRES ENERGY—KEEP IT UP

You don't have to be "all singing/all dancing" but you do, in effect, have to be captivating. You must keep the audience's attention. You can certainly use some of the techniques discussed in the sections of this book where we talk about how we conduct an interview and explain the importance of body language and such verbal cues as the pregnant pause and even softening your voice. Creating variety on stage stimulates an audience, keeps them interested, and therefore listening. It's not just about giving them what they want...it's more about giving them what you want.

The following is a checklist are good indicators as to whether you connected or didn't with the audience. Where did or do you fall with your presentation skills?

CONNECTORS:

◊ GOT THE AUDIENCE THINKING, AND REACTING, MOVED THE AUDIENCE IN A WAY TO CHEER

◊ SPEAKER WAS DYNAMIC

◊ Not flamboyant (unless that is your useful shtick) but captivating

◊ SHOWED GREAT SENSE OF CONFIDENCE

◊ INFORMATION SOUNDED NEW AND FRESH

◊ GAVE AUDIENCE:

   ◊ Ease

   ◊ Security

   ◊ Confidence

NON-CONNECTORS:

◊ MONOTONE VOICE
Were you bland on the ear...uninspiring to listen to?

◊ NO PASSION OR CONVICTION
People may only remember how you made them feel.

◊ NO CONTENT
Where were the anecdotes/examples/stories...facts and fig-ures can be boring.

◊   EMOTED NEGATIVE ATTITUDE
Body language like slouching or crossed arms can connote a
disconnect with the audience.

◊   SPOKE DOWN TO THE AUDIENCE
Coming across as someone who lauds over the audience that
you "know something they don't know" only makes you look
superior...and that makes the audience feel inferior.

THE ART OF SIMPLICITY

◊   TALK "TO" PEOPLE NOT "AT" THEM
There is a vast difference between the two. Again, you want
to connect with your audience, not strafe them with information or facts and leave them dead to your issue. You want
them to come along on the ride. If you disconnect... they
surely will.

◊   GET TO THE POINT
Make your point up front and then punctuate with anecdotes
and examples. If you start with the latter, your message may
seem meandering and get lost.

◊   REPEAT SO PEOPLE UNDERSTAND
Again, it is not redundant to repeat your message...it is down-
right mandatory to get it across. You don't have to use the
same verbiage, but you might emphasize a point. Alternatively, you can use colorful phrasing to say the same thing
differently if you feel repetition is not in the flow of the conversation.

◊   TALK CLEARLY
Remember, the point is to be understood not to simply fill
time. Clear talk is key to being understood.

◊   LESS IS MORE

You don't have to talk for the sake of talking. If you have said
enough…STOP. Your audience will appreciate you not wasting
their time. There is a difference between repeating the message to drive the point and browbeating. You don't want to
lose an audience or message because you angered the audience. It is worth practicing your speech several times—with
an audience and without to work out the timings and comfort
levels with delivery.

TAKE FEEDBACK

Feedback is your friend—both negative as well as positive. You may
learn far more from the negative than you ever will from being ego-
stroked by the positive. Look for constructive criticism. After all,
these people had invested their time in your appearance and you
either were worth the investment or not. You want to make sure you
are always worth their time and, perhaps, money. Having said that,
not all feedback may work for you. They simply may not have gotten
the presentation. But was that because they didn't understand you or
did you not deliver clearly to them? If you can honestly say, their criticism was far off base, so be it. Move on and don't let it shake you. If
you can find a grain of truth in what they've said, see if you can incorporate or make the necessary change to improve your performance
for the future. It is all good.

SIDEBAR: BREANA ROSS

*Breana Ross is a passionate journalist and servant leader who has
turned her passion for writing and public speaking into a nationally
growing, youth-oriented, organization: Written in My Soul—shar-
ing her love for poetry with youth and gives youth a way to express
their emotions healthily. Breana started the first chapter of Written
in My Soul on the University of Miami's campus in 2016. Breana is
currently a reporter at WBAL in Baltimore, MD where she reports on*

everything from social issues to crime to politics and education. She just started a chapter of Written in My Soul in Baltimore and engages with the community regularly by hosting and emceeing events.

Her most influential public speaking project came as Breana studied abroad in South Africa where she served in two different townships teaching kids reading and math after school. She spoke about her experiences serving in the United States and abroad during her TED Talk called "Impact Money Can't Buy"—which emphasizes how philanthropy can be more about service of time, contact, and gifts of talent rather than just money.

The process of creating a TED talk is a good model for addressing all public speaking options.

What was your first consideration?
"Length of time. I had up to twenty minutes, but I opted to stay around eleven, knowing I could hit all my points and be clear and concise without having to rush."

When did content come into consideration?
"Next. I wanted to create actionable content for the audience to walk away with empowerment. I made a list with an end goal. If I didn't feel like the content included something the audience could walk away with as a positive action for them to incorporate into their own lives, then it was cut. Self-editing is key and must be objective."

Is simply speaking enough?
"It can be but I don't ascribe to that idea. I added pictures, graphic words for punctuation, and anecdotes for engagement within the presentation. I believe you constantly have to keep the audience attentive and remind

them of the message."
Do you have a style and how important is it to define
that style?

Mine is conversational. Less formal. I work hard at not
coming across as a performer. But defining your style is
key to showing your audience your most authentic self.
And that is, after all, what they are there to see."
While her how-to is a basic bible for public speaking,
Breana also has the following tips:

- *USE STORYTELLING*
  You want to include both facts and, more im-
  portantly, feelings.

- *BE AS CONVERSATIONAL AS POSSIBLE*
  You want to come off as natural as you can
  be. But...being more conversational helps with
  nerves.

- *MAKE EYE CONTACT*
  Scan the room and try to create a moment
  with as many people as you can. It engages
  them. Also, create a focal point so you are not
  looking all over the place and appearing scat-
  tered.

- *DON'T USE NOTES... IF POSSIBLE*
  Memorize bullet points if you can. You don't
  have to be "on point" to make your point. It
  allows you to be more conversational, and
  free-flowing. Reading from notes can be dis-
  engaging for the audience.

- ***PREPARATION IS KEY***
  Practice, practice, practice! In front of family and friends or co-workers...and...in the mirror. Why the mirror? It is good to know what you look like in terms of body language and expression. You want to hone those skills as much as content.

FINAL THOUGHTS

FINAL THOUGHTS

THE THREE PHILOSOPHIES:
THAT HAVE NEVER STEERED ME WRONG:

And yes, they have been referred to before within these pages...they are worth reiterating...and remembering!

FIRST: I LIVE ON A TREE

Over the years, I have been asked to lecture at universities and inevitably the students want to place my career into a box...categorizing my vast accomplishments into one single entity: YOU ARE THIS! Well, the truth is, as the media evolves and morphs, you must as well. You may do THIS one day and need or want to do THAT the next. There is no harm or shame in changing direction as long as you don't change trajectory—that is the art of moving forward. So, when people ask how I describe who I am in the industry, I tell them that my career is a tree and at this particular time, I am sitting on THIS branch.

Entertainment is the tree—solid and made up of all your divergent skills. One day you may be a journalist and the next, you may be doing a podcast, and the next a brand influencer. All three of those important positions in your life may come as an offshoot of each other or happen at the same time as each other. Don't be afraid to multitask and hop from branch to branch. The value of that is multi-fold:

1. It broadens your skill sets.

2. It attracts a larger audience and/or following which is enticing to future employers, brands, and marketers.

3. It keeps you relevant across multiple platforms for marketability.

In today's marketplace, no matter what you do, you must have a social media presence. If you are a local journalist in even a small market town, you are expected at the very least to feed your stories to a Facebook page and have your own social media connections to where you can interact with viewers. That is happening more and more in the corporate world as well. (Take note all you realtors and lawyers out there.) That is why on page one of this book, I stated the lessons learned in this book are not luxuries...they are necessities.

The branch you are sitting on may not be the branch you end up on but realizing they all stem from a collective tree known as your career will give you overall focus and marketability. DON'T BE AFRAID TO BRANCH OUT!

SECOND: I PLAY A LOT OF DARTS

The students I speak to, as a good example, are very goal oriented. That is a good thing—as it should be. But don't be blinded by a goal. Do not necessarily use laser vision but rather use your peripheral vision to get where you want to go. And that begs for the analogy of the game of darts.

If you have ever played a game of darts, the board is set up with pie-sliced sections of point values of 1-20 respectively with a little red dot in the middle, the BULL'S EYE, which is the hardest to hit and valued at 50 points. To win the game, you must throw your pointed little missile darts at the board and accumulate 301 points.

Now in society, we have all heard the terms "going for the bull's eye", or "shoot for the bull's eye", or "aim for the bull's eye" and have translated this vernacular to mean we are going for the big prize, going for it all—that we have a goal in mind and we will settle for nothing less. Well, to win the game of darts you need 300+01 points to win. The bull's eye is worth 50 points. You could hit the bull's eye every time and NOT win the game...because you need that one extra single point to win. You must play the board.

That is my analogy. You must play the board. It is good to have an eye on the bull's eye for your career goal but it is what is on the board around it that will help you win the game. Perhaps, in playing the board, you may never need the bull's eye at all and you still come out a winner. And here is an example of how that works.

One day you may start out thinking about being a radio broadcaster... but to get there you create a podcast. That podcast may lead you to radio or it may be successful in its own right and lead you to television commentary or social media influencing and so on. Focus on the goal, that is your bullseye...but...USE YOUR PERIPHERAL VISION to get there!

THIRD: I ONLY SELL BROWN SHOES

Remember you are not a person; you are a product. We've talked about this, again in the opening pages. You can't take the negative feedback as a personal attack—it is a reaction to the product. To that end, you want to market that product in its best possible light to the broadest possible audience. And there is no getting around it, it takes a clever mind and determination—like any success story. Commitment!

But if you ever feel lost in the process, remember the perspective in which I always place it. When people ask what I do...and I am feeling just a little snarky...I tell them: "I sell brown shoes!" The truth is, I do. My job is to sell brown shoes (me) in an industry where everyone is wearing black shoes (the competition). And once I convince them (the buyer of the product—me) that brown is the new black.

I have to convince them that I am the only one they should buy from.

The analogy is the shame, shoes or media...you or the next guy.
No one said this was going to be easy...but even the journey can be
fun. Remember the pie is always big enough for you to take a slice
too.

MIC DROP!

NOTES: